CARLTON **FOOD** NETWORK

D0657759

The
WINTER NOSH
Nosh
Brothers

CFN CARLTON **FOOD** NETWORK From the hit TV series

First published in 1997 by HarperCollins*Publishers*

A catalogue record for this book is available from the British Library.

ISBN 0 00 414041 9

For HarperCollins*Publishers*

Commissioning editor: Barbara Dixon

Designed and produced by SP Creative Design

Editor: Heather Thomas

Designer: Al Rockall

Art Director: Rolando Ugolini

Photography

Food photographs: Sue Atkinson

Photographs of the Nosh Brothers: Tony Latham

Colour origination and printing by The Bath Press

CARLTON **FOOD** NETWORK

Whether you live to eat or eat to live, Carlton Food Network has something to tempt your tastebuds. Europe's only dedicated food channel brings the expertise of the world's finest chefs, food experts and celebrities to television screens throughout the country.

Carlton Food Network provides an exciting range of programmes featuring celebrity chefs and personalities such as The Nosh Brothers, Brian Turner, Antony Worrall Thompson, Paul Gayler, Ross Burden, Nanette Newman and many more.

There is something on offer for all food lovers: the great programme line-up features a host of shows presented by the country's top chefs, as well as food from every corner of the world – Africa, India, Italy, China, Scotland, England and Ireland, to mention but a few!

The Carlton Food Network has dedicated itself to ensuring that you know all there is to know about healthy eating and nutrition — so you really can enjoy what you eat. Kids can also try out their culinary skills as the Carlton Food Network features some tasty recipes in a children's programme — and find out how to grow the freshest ingredients to use in the kitchen with the Carlton Food Network's very own gardening slot!

In short, the Carlton Food Network has an exciting mix of ingredients which will appeal to all tastebuds!

Tune into Carlton Food Network, TV's tastiest channel for recipes to make your mouth water.

THE AUTHORS

Mick and Nick Nosh are hosting their new TV series, *Winter Nosh*, on the Carlton Food Network. This follows their hugely popular barbecuing series, *Red Hot & Smokin'*. Before starting their business collaboration in 1992, they both enjoyed successful careers in the media, music and entertainment industries, having served their apprenticeships in famous kitchens around the world.

In 1993 they opened their own restaurant in London's Fulham Road, serving the type of food they wanted to eat, in the surroundings in which they wanted to eat, with the food served as they wanted it to be served.

Renowned for their celebrity parties and successful restaurant, their reputation for first-class entertaining and sensational, honest 'food with attitude' rapidly grew, winning them widespread critical acclaim.

They have made extensive magazine, television and radio appearances, hosted a Talk Radio food and drink programme, and have written a book on *Entertaining* (published by Macmillan).

IMPORTANT NOTE

Please note that all the recipes appearing in this book serve eight people, unless otherwise specified. To serve less people, adjust the quantities accordingly.

ACKNOWLEDGEMENTS

We are indebted to the following for assistance and inspiration in the preparation of this book: Aunt Bente, Michele Van Bloepol and the family Nosh, Mothers N & M, Father M. Nosh, Viscount Edward, Kevin, and Uncle Mortimer.

CONTENTS

INTRODUCTION

The essence of winter food is to make a contrast in our diet to the lighter food we've been eating during the summer. Generally speaking, we feel the need to eat warmer and heavier food. However, this doesn't mean that one has to swallow stodge until the clocks change back again. This book, *Winter Nosh*, contains not only nourishing and tasty dishes, but also some old favourites that we have given a fashionable twist in our own inimitable style.

All the ingredients for the dishes are available from a good supermarket so you should have no worries about sourcing ingredients. Our creations are written in a simple-to-read, non-jargon manner and have no need of any specialist kitchen equipment.

To make life easy for you we have specified that all recipes are for eight people. Having experienced many different vogues in food in recent years, this book brings back some of the retro style, again with the Nosh Brothers' spin.

In certain recipes, we have not specified the accompanying side dishes of vegetables — we feel that this can be left to individual taste. Where we have mentioned specific vegetable methods, it is to introduce you to our own distinctive way of presenting these complementary dishes.

However, beware that one of the past traditions in this country is to boil vegetables to death, rendering them a tasteless and colourless mush with no appeal. Many of our seasonal winter vegetables can be almost a meal in themselves, and we often cook specific vegetables not just in salted water but in a light chicken stock, which can add a wonderful flavour.

One of the benefits of the seasonality of these dishes is that they can be prepared in advance which thereby allows you to wrap up warmly and have time for a brisk walk to the pub. Stews and casseroles, particularly, are improved by resting, their flavours blending and mingling well to give a better result.

starters

FISH SOUP WITH ROUILLE TOASTS

CLAM AND MUSSEL SOUP

ONION SOUP WITH GRUYERE TOASTS

THAI CHICKEN SOUP

CAULIFLOWER SOUP

PEA AND HAM SOUP

WILD MUSHROOM SOUP

MINESTRONE SOUP

PRAWN COCKTAIL

THAI FISHCAKES ON MANGO SALAD

GRILLED GOAT'S CHEESE SALAD

CHICKEN BROTH WITH MEATBALLS

ONION BHAJIS WITH
MANGO CHUTNEY

WARM SALAD OF CHICKEN LIVERS
WITH A POACHED EGG

SPICY PORK WITH SPINACH

GARLIC STUFFED FIELD MUSHROOMS

HOT POTATO SALAD WITH
BACON AND EGG

FISH SOUP
WITH ROUILLE TOASTS

See photograph opposite page 16.

FOR THE SOUP

2 red peppers, cored and deseeded

2 large Spanish onions, peeled

2 fennel bulbs, with feathery tops

1 old potato, peeled

6 tablespoons olive oil

4 garlic cloves, peeled and crushed

450 g/1 lb mussels, cleaned and bearded

675 g/1 1/2 lb mixed white fish

1 prepared crab

450 g/1 lb fresh squid, prepared

2.4 litres/4 pints rich fish stock (see opposite)

1 teaspoon saffron strands

sea salt and freshly ground black pepper

grated Gruyère (or Parmesan) cheese, to serve

a small dash of chilli sherry

A rich and filling soup, this can be served as a robust main course if the bowl is big enough. Slurp it and imagine that you are by the harbourside in Vieilles Antibes on the Riviera!

SOUP: Chop all the vegetables finely and sauté slowly in the olive oil over a low heat for 20 minutes, until soft. Then add the garlic, the mussels (discarding the shells when opened), the white fish, crab flesh and squid. Continue cooking for another 5 minutes.

Next, pour the fish stock over the fish and vegetable mixture, add the saffron, and simmer for about 30 minutes. Season and then liquidize the soup and keep warm.

TOASTS: Mix the rouille ingredients together. Toast the bread slices and spread the rouille on the toasted baguette rounds. Float the rouille toasts in the soup, with a sprinkling of grated Gruyère (or Parmesan) on top. Add a dash of chilli sherry.

STOCK: Just about any fish is suitable apart from very oily fish, such as mackerel, tuna, etc. The only advice here is to remove any gills with stout scissors, as these sometimes give a bitter flavour to the stock — although fiddly, it's worth the effort.

Put all the ingredients into a large saucepan and bring to the boil. Skim off any scum or froth and discard it. Lower the heat to a slow simmer and cook the bones for about 45 minutes, continuing to skim as necessary. Pass the liquid through a fine metal sieve or some muslin to strain it, and discard the bones, fish heads, etc. Then return the liquid to the pan and reduce it by at least one-quarter on a fast boil so that you end up with 1.8 litres/3 pints of well-flavoured stock.

You can make the stock up to three days beforehand and keep it chilled in the fridge, or it can be frozen for up to three months. Warm before using.

CHILLI SHERRY

This culinary secret was shown to Mick by some local Maltese chefs as a good way of livening up fish soups. It's also become a Nosh tradition for sharpening up Bloody Marys.

Into a sterilized white wine (clear glass) bottle place 4 large whole fresh red chillies (previously blanched for 15 seconds in boiling water). Pour over them a bottle of dry sherry. Use something like a fino; cream or medium sherries do not seem to work so well. Leave to steep for about three weeks and you can pour a few drops into risottos, gravies, soups and many sauces.

FOR THE ROUILLE TOASTS

4 tablespoons fresh mayonnaise (see page 23)

3 hard-boiled egg yolks, mashed

2 garlic cloves, peeled and pulped

a generous pinch of cayenne pepper

1 baguette, cut into rounds, toasted

FOR THE STOCK

2.25 kg/5 lb mixed fish bones, salmon heads etc.

1 large Spanish onion, sliced

4 carrots, peeled

1 fennel bulb with feathery top, thickly sliced

1.8 litres/3 pints water

4 black peppercorns

1 bottle light white wine

225 g/8 oz mushrooms

1 bouquet garni

CLAM AND
MUSSEL SOUP

INGREDIENTS

150 g/5 oz unsalted butter

175 g/6 oz onions, chopped

175 g/6 oz shallots, chopped

250 g/10 oz white leeks, cleaned and chopped

1 kg/2 lb 2 oz fresh mussels

1 kg/2 lb 2 oz fresh clams

3 bouquets garni

1/2 teaspoon ground white pepper

225 ml/8 fl oz dry white wine

2 garlic cloves, chopped

225 g/8 oz tomatoes, peeled and chopped

225 g/8 oz carrots, diced

1 stalk celery, chopped

1/2 bulb fennel, chopped

1.5 litres/2 1/2 pints fish stock (see page 11)

large pinch of saffron

300 ml/1/2 pint double cream

sea salt and ground black pepper

chopped chervil, to serve

Mussels are the most under-rated, inexpensive shellfish — and long may they remain so! Releasing copious amounts of liquids, they very kindly make their own sauce — all we have to do is flavour it!

Mussels are filter feeders and if kept cool they will have their shells shut. If left to warm up out of the water, their shells will open, and that potentially is where the possibility of contamination lies. Hence the old maxim — only eat mussels, oysters, etc. when there is an 'R' in the month, i.e. in cool weather.

METHOD: Heat 2 teaspoons of butter in a large saucepan and sweat one-third of the onions, shallots and leeks over a low heat. Add the mussels, clams, one bouquet garni and white pepper together with the white wine, and agitate the pan to allow all the mussels to receive heat on the bottom layer.

When all the mussels are opened (discarding, as usual, all unopened 'dead' shellfish), drain off the liquor into a bowl and reserve, then remove the shellfish meat from their shells, removing any stray 'beards'. Set aside.

Heat the remaining butter in a large saucepan and sweat off the remaining leeks, onions and shallots with the garlic, chopped tomatoes, diced carrots, celery and fennel. Add the other bouquets garni and cook for 5 minutes. Add the fish stock and reserved mussel/clam liquor and bring to the boil.

Keep some clams and mussels for garnishing the soup and put the rest with the saffron into the pot to simmer for 20 minutes. Remove the bouquets garni, then add the double cream, and pour into a processor or blender and whizz until smooth.

Adjust the seasoning and return to the saucepan to heat through gently. Serve with a sprinkling of chopped chervil and the reserved mussel and clam garnish.

So good, you'll eat it when there's an 'R' in the month... and an 'E', and an 'A', and...

NOSH TIP

You can 'fatten up' the mussels when you get them back home by simply placing them in some cold salted water you have made up (you will need approximately 4 handfuls of salt per 2-gallon bucket of cold fresh water) and stirring in some oatmeal, which has previously been blitzed in a blender on high speed for a few seconds, or some plain flour. If left for a few hours or even overnight, the shellfish will filter feed, and this has the effect of allowing them to 'clean' themselves and fatten themselves up for cooking!

ONION SOUP
WITH GRUYERE TOASTS

FOR THE SOUP

900 g/2 lb Spanish onions, thinly sliced

1 tablespoon olive oil

50 g/2 oz unsalted butter

1 teaspoon sea salt

freshly ground black pepper

1 teaspoon caster sugar

1 tablespoon plain flour

1 large glass (350 ml/12 fl oz) white wine

2 litres/3½ pints beef stock (see page 43)

2 tablespoons Armagnac

FOR THE GRUYÈRE TOASTS

cut discs of baguette, 5 mm/¼ in thick

225 g/8 oz finely grated Gruyère cheese

The secret to a sweet rich flavour is to sauté the onions very slowly and then simmer also, for a very long time. Don't try to rush this part — it won't pay dividends.

METHOD: Sauté the sliced onions in the olive oil and butter in a heavy-bottomed, cast-iron casserole pot. Sweat them for at least 15 minutes over a low heat, with the lid on the pot. Then turn up the heat to a medium-high temperature, add the salt, a good grinding of black pepper and the sugar and cook, stirring frequently, until the onions brown slightly but retain some of their translucence. Do not allow them to become burnt — this will affect their taste. The whole process will take at least 30 minutes so don't try to hurry it.

Sift the flour over the cooked onion mass and continue frying for a minute, stirring well to prevent the onions sticking. Next, add the wine and beef stock and stir well to break up any lumps of flour.

Bring back to the boil and simmer for 40 minutes, until all the onions are 'melt-in-the-mouth' soft. Then add the Armagnac. Pour some soup into each heatproof bowl, float a few toasts, well-loaded with grated Gruyère, on top and place under a hot grill for a few minutes to melt the cheese. Serve the soup immediately before the bread starts to get soaked and sink.

THAI
CHICKEN SOUP

What is more warming than spicy food in winter? Tom Ka Gai is the celebrated Thai chicken and coconut sour soup. Here we show you how to make one of our most sustaining starters. A little chilli goes a long way, so don't overdo the heat — but don't stint on it either. This soup is famously hot and you should get a little sweat on with this one!

METHOD: Heat the chicken stock in a large saucepan. Add the lime leaves, lemon grass, ginger, fish sauce and lemon juice. Stir and bring to the boil.

Add the sliced chicken and coconut milk, then reduce the heat to a simmer. Cook gently for about 3 minutes, until the chicken is cooked through. Add the chillies and pour into small bowls. Garnish with coriander leaves and serve immediately.

NOSH TIP

When using lemon grass, be sure to remove the coarse outer leaves. This is a typical fiery Thai soup and it is designed to be very strongly flavoured. If you have a delicate palate, reduce the chilli quota.

FOR THE SOUP

1.5 litres/2^{1}/$_{2}$ pints chicken stock

6 lime leaves, chopped

3 x 10-cm/4-in pieces lemon grass, chopped

1 x 7.5-cm/3-in piece fresh root ginger, peeled and thinly sliced

12 tablespoons fish sauce

10 tablespoons lemon juice

350 g/12 oz skinned, boned chicken breast, thinly sliced

600 ml/1 pint thick coconut milk

6 small red chillies, sliced thinly diagonally

handful of chopped fresh coriander, to serve

CAULIFLOWER
SOUP

INGREDIENTS

1 large fresh cauliflower

2 medium onions, chopped

4 tablespoons olive oil

50 g/2 oz slightly salted butter

1 large 'old' potato, finely grated (to thicken the soup)

1.2 litres/2 pints fresh chicken stock (a good quality stock cube will do)

300 ml/¹/₂ pint whole milk

sea salt and white pepper

This is an unusual soup with a delicate flavour and interesting texture. The main thing is to take care not to overheat it as it will 'split' and look odd.

METHOD: Prepare the cauliflower by removing the outer leaves, cutting it in half and removing the hard central stalk. Chop the florets into small pieces. Sauté the onions gently in the olive oil and butter without browning them. When the onions have softened, add the chopped cauliflower, grated potato and chicken stock. Bring to the boil, then reduce the heat and simmer for 15 minutes.

Process the soup in batches in a blender or food processor — it should not be too fine. Then return the puréed soup to a saucepan and add the milk and season to taste. Heat through very gently for 5 minutes at a bare simmer to prevent the milk splitting. Allow to cool slightly — for about 5 minutes — and then serve the soup with some crusty bread.

" The key to a good cauliflower soup is top-quality chicken stock. Don't stint on this. And don't let anyone give you a vegetarian version — it doesn't have the guts! "

Opposite: Fish soup with rouille toasts (page 10).

PEA AND HAM
SOUP

This is one of the most warming and satisfying of all winter soups. As gammon is a heavily salt-cured meat, there should be no need to add any salt to this recipe. Check the seasoning at the end.

STOCK: Cut some of the meat off the gammon bone and cut into thin strips. Reserve for the garnish. Put the vegetables, parsley and gammon bone pieces into a large pot with the water and wine vinegar. Bring to the boil, then skim off any scum from the surface and reduce the heat to a slow simmer. Cook gently, uncovered, for at least 1 hour, skimming off scum as necessary. Strain the liquid through a very fine mesh filter into a jug or basin.

SOUP: Sweat the onions, carrots and celery in the oil and butter for about 5 minutes, until soft. Add the split peas, gammon stock and white pepper. Cook slowly over a very low heat for about 45 minutes, stirring occasionally.

Blitz the soup in a food processor on high speed, for a few short bursts, to pulverize it, or sieve through a mouli. There should be some grainy texture to this rustic recipe so don't overdo the blender time. If wished, the soup can be thinned down with milk. Return to the rinsed-out pan, heat through and season with black pepper. Serve in hot bowls garnished with the reserved ham strips. Swirl in some soured cream and sprinkle with parsley.

Opposite: Thai fishcakes on mango salad (page 24).

FOR THE SOUP

2 large onions, finely chopped

2 large carrots, finely chopped

2 sticks celery, peeled and chopped

4 tablespoons oil

50 g/2 oz unsalted butter

900 g/2 lb green split peas, soaked overnight and drained

ground white pepper

freshly ground black pepper

150 ml/1/4 pint soured cream

finely chopped parsley, to serve

FOR THE STOCK

1 large gammon bone, with some meat attached, cut in 4 sections

2 large carrots, chopped

1 onion, chopped

2 large leeks, chopped

small bunch of parsley, chopped

2.4 litres/4 pints water

1 tablespoon white wine vinegar

WILD
MUSHROOM SOUP

INGREDIENTS

500 g/1 lb 2 oz closed cup field mushrooms

300 g/10 oz selection of wild mushrooms

1 large Spanish (mild) onion, very finely chopped

1 tablespoon olive oil

75 g (3 oz) unsalted butter

1 garlic clove, crushed

1.2 litres/2 pints chicken stock (see opposite)

300 ml/¹/₂ pint whole milk

sea salt and freshly ground black pepper

¹/₂ teaspoon freshly grated nutmeg

300 ml/¹/₂ pint single cream

4 tablespoons chopped fresh parsley

Although most English people have no idea about how to recognise an edible wild mushroom, these days, many supermarkets have a reasonable selection on offer. If you want to go out and find some yourself, take a wise expert who will identify the good ones for you — you don't want to injure yourself. There are some good illustrated guides on identification — we recommend that you study them carefully before embarking on a hunt.

METHOD: Clean the fungi with a pastry brush (rinse if necessary), and allow to drain. Chop all the fungi, except 115 g/4 oz of the wild selection, reserving this for the garnish. (These can be sweated off separately in a little olive oil and, when tender, allowed to cool.)

Sweat the onion in the olive oil and butter in a large saucepan for 6 minutes over a low to medium flame, stirring to prevent catching and sticking. You should achieve a light golden transparent colour. Add the mushrooms and garlic and sauté along with the onions over a high heat. The juices released by the mushrooms will prevent the onions becoming over-coloured. Add the chicken stock when the juices are starting to dry up, and cook for 10 minutes on a slow simmer. Then add the milk, bring back to the boil and simmer for another 5 minutes. Adjust the seasoning, with salt, pepper and nutmeg, and whizz the whole lot through a processor until the soup has a smooth to medium texture. It should be able to be spooned easily but not so smooth that it resembles baby food.

Serve in warmed bowls with a swirl of fresh single cream and a spoonful of the reserved fried wild mushrooms in the centre for a garnish. Sprinkle with finely chopped parsley.

CHICKEN STOCK: Put the chicken bones and trimmings in a large stockpot with all the ingredients down to and including the white wine. Bring to the boil, and boil for 15–20 minutes, until the wine has nearly evaporated. Add the cold water, the herbs, bouquet garni and spices, and bring back to the boil. Simmer for 1 1/2 hours, skimming the surface frequently with a ladle to remove any scummy froth. When cooked, strain through a fine conical strainer. Now transfer the stock to a clean saucepan and place on a high heat to boil and reduce the stock by at least half its volume to render it strong tasting. You should end up with at least 1.2 litres/2 pints of well-flavoured liquid.

NOSH TIP

Try to choose, if possible, varieties of mushrooms that will not discolour the soup (i.e. no amethyst deceiver, black trompettes, etc.); opt for plenty of light-coloured fungi, such as girolles, cèpes, chanterelles, etc.

FOR THE CHICKEN STOCK

1.1 kg/2 1/2 lb chicken carcass bones and trimmings/giblets

450 g/1 lb chicken wings and trimmings

50 g/2 oz streaky bacon, chopped

115 g/4 oz carrots, finely diced

115 g/4 oz mushrooms, finely diced

115 g/4 oz onion, finely diced

225 g/8 oz leek, finely diced

2 fresh tomatoes, deseeded and skinned

1 shallot, chopped

2 garlic cloves, crushed

600 ml/1 pint white wine

2.3 litres/4 pints cold water

a bunch of parsley stalks

a pinch each of dried tarragon and chervil

1 bouquet garni (thyme, parsley, bay leaf, etc.)

6 black peppercorns

2 cloves

MINESTRONE
SOUP

FOR THE SOUP

3 onions, sliced

75 g/3 oz chopped lardons of smoked streaky bacon

50 g/2 oz unsalted butter

4 large carrots, diced

3 celery sticks, diced

1 leek, cleaned and finely chopped

150 g/5 oz dried Borlotti beans, soaked overnight

115 g/4 oz French beans, trimmed and diced

2 medium courgettes, diced

115 g/4 oz shelled peas

3 garlic cloves, crushed

175 g/6 oz Savoy cabbage, shredded

2.4 litres/4 pints strong meat stock (or 4 good bouillon cubes)

1 glass white wine

225 g/8 oz tomatoes, blanched and peeled (canned tomatoes will do)

Many variations exist on this central theme of a thick vegetable soup, simmered for a long time in a meat stock. This is based on a Milanese-type soup with potato — and a little rice replacing the pasta — with the addition of a generous spoonful of pesto (alla Genovese) just before serving.

SOUP: Sauté the onions and bacon in the butter in a heavy-based casserole pot over a medium heat for 5 minutes. Then add the carrots, celery and leek and sweat for a few minutes. Add the drained, soaked Borlotti beans, sauté for another 5 minutes and then add the French beans, courgettes, peas and garlic. Lastly add the cabbage and sweat off for another 5 minutes. Then add the strong meat stock, white wine, tomatoes, seasoning and herbs and bring the soup to the boil. Reduce the heat to very low and simmer gently for about 2–3 hours. Add the potatoes and rice after $2^1/_2$ hours.

The cooking should be very gentle so that each small cube of vegetable retains its shape and does not become mushy, but the juices add to the taste of the soup.

Serve the soup sprinkled with freshly grated Parmesan and chopped parsley and hand round the pesto sauce separately for guests to help themselves. Stirring a little of this vibrant sauce into the soup will add a delicious flavour.

PESTO SAUCE: Remove the basil leaves from the stems and, handling them as little as possible to prevent them bruising and blackening, place in a mortar (or processor) and blend with the nuts, garlic and oil — adding the oil gradually, a little at a time. (In a processor, you'll have to scrape down the sides of the bowl with a spatula after 10 seconds and process for another 10 seconds.) Then add the seasonings and the cheeses and blend to combine. Cover and refrigerate for an hour to let the flavours develop.

The best basil in Italy is reputed to come from Liguria, but others will suffice. Don't over-season your pesto as it is impossible to adjust it or rectify it once it has gone wrong.

NOSH TIP

If you can't get Pecorino cheese for the pesto sauce, grated Gruyère makes a fine-tasting substitute. You can use a food processor to make the sauce but the best results are obtained by using an old-fashioned pestle and mortar.

Soup continued

sea salt and ground black pepper

1 bay leaf

small pinch of Provençal herbs

400 g/14 oz floury 'old' potatoes, cut in half

150 g/5 oz risotto rice

75 g/3 oz freshly grated Parmesan

chopped parsley and pesto sauce, to serve

FOR THE PESTO SAUCE

1 large bunch fresh basil leaves

50 g/2 oz toasted pine nuts

25 g/1 oz shelled walnuts, chopped

2 garlic cloves, chopped

175 ml/6 fl oz virgin olive oil

sea salt and ground black pepper

25 g/1 oz finely grated Pecorino cheese

25 g/1 oz finely grated Parmesan

PRAWN COCKTAIL

40 large fresh-cooked prawns, head on, middle section shelled

fresh chilled crisp Cos lettuce

fresh lime wedges, to serve

150 ml/¼ pint freshly made thick mayonnaise

6 tablespoons tomato sauce (see opposite)

4 tablespoons double cream

1 tablespoon anchovy or Worcestershire sauce

juice of 1 lime or ½ lemon

small amount (8 large leaves) chopped basil

large dash of Tabasco sauce or chilli sherry (see page 11)

P*rawn cocktail is a well designed starter that everyone knows became a byword for 'naff' in the sophisticated Eighties, being associated with the well-done steak and Black Forest gâteau. This was mostly because of indifferent hotel catering or cheap and nasty wine bars that pre-prepared wine glasses full of indifferent sauce ladled on top of waterlogged thawed prawns with brown-tinged iceberg lettuce. Now it has undergone something of a fashionable renaissance in certain circles — which is, we think, perfectly OK so long as the ingredients are not stinted on.*

PRAWN COCKTAIL: Prepare the mayonnaise and tomato sauce, then mix in the remaining cocktail sauce ingredients. Take eight 20-cm/8-in diameter oriental soup bowls (or other wide bowls) and arrange the larger Cos lettuce leaves around the sides of each bowl. Fill with some shredded leaves to form a base. Spoon on some of the creamy cocktail sauce and place 5 large prawns around the edge of each bowl. Hang some wedges of fresh lime on the sides of the bowl for squeezing.

TOMATO SAUCE: Pass the tomatoes through a fine mouli sieve to remove the seeds and skin. Heat the olive oil in a solid-based saucepan over a medium heat and add the onion, garlic, basil, oregano and white pepper. Stir briskly to prevent the onion browning. When the onion has softened, add the tomato pulp.

Bring the mixture to the boil and immediately reduce the heat to a low simmer. Remove the garlic and basil stems and discard.

Stir in the sugar (this balances the acidity of the tomatoes) and a little salt. Simmer the sauce for about 30 minutes, until well reduced. The solids will tend to condense on the bottom of the pan, so stir with a wooden spoon occasionally. The time taken will vary, depending on the degree of wateriness of the original canned tomato contents, so keep an eye on the pan. Season the finished sauce with freshly ground black pepper and salt if needed.

MAYONNAISE

Whisk 3 small fresh egg yolks and 1 tablespoon white wine vinegar with some sea salt and 1 teaspoon good-quality Dijon mustard. Mix together 150 ml/^{1}/4 pint good olive oil and 300 ml/^{1}/2 pint good sunflower oil. Drizzle in the mixed oils, incorporating them thoroughly, beating all the time, until half of the oil is used. Then add 1 teaspoon lemon juice and continue to pour and whisk in the oils. Finally, adjust the seasoning to taste and add a pinch of caster sugar..

If the resulting mayo either looks too thin or has split or curdled, it is possible to rescue it by beating another yolk in a separate bowl and pouring the original mixture in gradually, beating well as before, but really taking plenty of time to whisk well together.

FOR THE TOMATO SAUCE

2 x 400-g/14-oz cans Italian plum tomatoes with their juices

50 ml/2 fl oz olive oil

^{1}/2 medium Spanish onion, finely chopped

2 large garlic cloves

^{1}/2 small bunch fresh sweet basil, about 12 g/^{1}/2 oz

^{1}/2 tablespoon fresh or dried oregano

pinch of ground white pepper

1 teaspoon caster sugar

sea salt

freshly ground black pepper

IMPORTANT TIP

To remove the worries and fears about any lurking salmonella in raw egg, simply mix the broken yolks with the vinegar at the start and leave for 5–10 minutes, stirring once or twice. Salmonella hate vinegar and it will reduce the risk of any contamination.

THAI FISHCAKES
ON MANGO SALAD

See photograph opposite page 17.

Spicy food goes a long way — these Thai fishcakes are easy to make, and the mix can be frozen, uncooked, for another day, if desired. Remember, though, the mangoes must be firm, not mushy, for a good result.

SALAD: Line a serving dish with the Chinese leaves. Combine all the ingredients, starting with the 'hardest' and then adding the liquids. Blend gently, but do not 'mush' them together. This strong

FOR THE SALAD

Chinese leaves, coarsely chopped

450 g/1 lb firm mango, grated on a mandolin 'julienne' setting (or use papaya)

225 g/8 oz cucumber julienne

115 g/4 oz carrot julienne

4 small garlic cloves

4 tablespoons coarsely ground roasted peanuts

4 tablespoons dried shrimp, ground coarsely

2 small red chillies, deseeded and chopped

4 tomatoes, sliced

4 tablespoons palm sugar (or soft brown)

8 tablespoons fish sauce

8 tablespoons lime juice

chopped mint and coriander leaves

NAM PLA SAUCE

Heat 4 tablespoons peanut oil in a small pan and fry 12 chopped shallots until crisp and brown. Remove with a slotted spoon and set aside.

Pour off most of the oil to leave a light film on the pan and then return half of the cooked shallots with 2 large garlic cloves, 4 deseeded and chopped chillies and 4 tablespoons each of fish sauce, palm sugar, lime juice and chicken stock. Stir until the mixture becomes syrupy and the sugar has melted, then add the remaining shallots. Remove from the heat and use as a warm dressing for the fishcakes.

liquid draws juices from the salad materials, so do not prepare the salad until the last minute before you need it.

FISHCAKES: Place all the ingredients except the fish, squid, prawns and oil, in a large food processor bowl and blend until well mixed. Add the fish, squid and prawns, and process quickly. Transfer the fish mixture to a bowl, cover with clingfilm and leave to rest in the refrigerator for 1 hour. This allows the flavours to mingle and develop.

Shape the mixture into small patties and fry in 3 mm/$^{1}/_8$ in oil in a frying pan over a medium heat until both sides are lightly browned. You can prepare all the fishcakes in this way before the meal, and then it only remains to place them on a foil-covered baking tray in a preheated medium-hot oven at 180°C/350°F/Gas Mark 4 for 4–5 minutes, until cooked right through.

Serve the fishcakes on a bed of mango salad with an accompanying dressing of Nam Pla sauce.

FOR THE FISHCAKES

1 egg

175 ml/6 fl oz thick coconut cream

1 red pepper, deseeded and finely chopped

50 g /2 oz thin green beans, trimmed and finely chopped

1 teaspoon green or red Thai curry paste

3 peeled lemon grass sticks (soft core only)

6 lime leaves, finely chopped

1 small red chilli, deseeded and finely chopped

sea salt

675 g/1$^{1}/_2$ lb white fish fillets, e.g. cod, skinned, boned and cut into chunks

225 g/8 oz squid, cleaned and chopped

115 g/4 oz green prawns, peeled and chopped

sunflower or peanut oil for frying

GRILLED GOAT'S
CHEESE SALAD

8 rounds of thinly sliced white bread

8 x 1-cm/¹/₂-in thick slices goat's cheese

mixed salad leaves, e.g. Batavia, Romaine, lamb's lettuce, frisée, oak leaf

8 small leeks, washed and trimmed

olive oil, for brushing

150 ml/¹/₄ pint French dressing made with mustard

4 spring onions, chopped

16 cherry tomatoes

freshly ground black pepper

French chèvre is quite good for this recipe, and the small barrel-shaped crottins are firm for slicing. However, there are now some magnificent British versions that are worth seeking out.

METHOD: Cut the white bread into rounds, slightly larger than the cheese discs. Toast them lightly and place on a baking tray. Put a cheese slice on each piece of toast and set aside in the fridge.

Wash and trim the salad leaves, tearing them into smallish pieces. Remove the green flags from the trimmed leeks and blanch them in gently boiling salted water for about 3 minutes to soften them. Drain thoroughly in a colander, 'tops down' to let the water run out. Heat a ridged griddle pan and paint a little olive oil on the hot surface. Grill each leek lightly until it has brown chargrill-type marks on each side. Place the leeks, side by side, in a baking dish and pour over the mustard dressing. The hot leeks will absorb some of the dressing. Allow to cool.

Mix the chopped spring onions with the tomatoes and salad leaves, and pour over some of the dressing from the leeks. Arrange in neat piles on serving plates. Split each leek down the centre with a sharp knife and place a strip on either side of the salads.

Grill the goat's cheese discs under a preheated hot grill until the top goes brown in places. Arrange on top of the salads with the remaining grilled leeks and a good grinding of black pepper to complete the dish.

CHICKEN BROTH
WITH MEATBALLS

This light starter benefits from making the stock at home from scratch. It has its roots in central Europe, and many versions abound in Spanish, German, French, Italian and Jewish cuisines, amongst others.

STOCK: Brown the carcasses in a preheated oven at 200°C/400°F/Gas Mark 6 for 15–20 minutes. Place them in a large pot with the giblets, vegetables, garlic and wine. Bring to the boil and continue boiling until the wine has nearly evaporated. Add 2–4 litres/4 pints of cold water with the remaining ingredients and bring to the boil. Simmer for 3 hours, skimming off any scum frequently.

Strain through a fine conical strainer and transfer the strained stock to a clean saucepan. Boil to reduce the stock by at least half of its volume to render it strong tasting. You should end up with 1.5 litres/2¹/₂ pints.

BROTH: Mix the beef and onion together, season and shape into small balls. Add to the hot stock with the carrots, spring onions and vermicelli. Simmer for about 5–10 minutes, until the carrots, meatballs and pasta are cooked. Season to taste and serve sprinkled with chopped parsley.

FOR THE BROTH

225 g/8 oz ground beef or veal

1 onion, finely grated

sea salt and ground black pepper

2 carrots, cut in julienne strips

1 bunch spring onions, chopped

75 g/3 oz vermicelli pasta

chopped parsley, to garnish

FOR THE STOCK

1.3 kg/2¹/₂ lb chicken carcasses

225 g/8 oz chicken giblets

115 g/4 oz carrots, diced

115 g/4 oz mushrooms, diced

115 g/4 oz onion, diced

115 g/4 oz leek, diced

2 tomatoes, deseeded

1 shallot, chopped

2 garlic cloves, crushed

600 ml/1 pint white wine

bunch of parsley stalks

1 bouquet garni

6 black peppercorns

ONION BHAJIS
WITH MANGO CHUTNEY

FOR THE BHAJIS

350 g/12 oz Gram (chickpea) flour

225 g/8 oz plain wheatflour

25 g/1 oz cumin seeds

2 small green chillies, deseeded and finely chopped

1 teaspoon sea salt

1/2 teaspoon cayenne pepper

1 teaspoon turmeric

300 ml/1/2 pint water, for batter

1.4 kg/3 lb Spanish onions, peeled and finely sliced

peanut oil for deep frying

lemon wedges, to serve

crisp lettuce leaves

Our ancestor Edward Nosh (renowned for his kedgeree secrets) smuggled a couple of his favourite bhajis out of India to reproduce the recipe at home in Europe. Unfortunately, he ate the samples before the train arrived at his destination, but we saved the recipe for posterity.

BHAJIS: Mix the flours, cumin seeds, chillies, sea salt, cayenne pepper and turmeric together until fully combined and then add the water, stirring until you have a stiff mixture. Add the finely sliced onions and let the batter rest for 5 minutes.

Take a serving spoon of the bhaji mixture and pat it down slightly to form an elegant patty, about the size of a whole fresh lime. Meanwhile, heat the peanut oil for deep frying until medium-hot — drop in a small blob of bhaji mixture off a spoon to test the temperature of the oil. The oil should be at about 160°C, which should cook the bhajis through in about 2–3 minutes each side. Drop a few bhajis at a time into the hot oil and fry until crisp and golden, turning halfway through. Serve the bhajis with lemon wedges and the mango chutney on a bed of crisp lettuce. Four each should make a decent starter.

CHUTNEY: Fry the spices and shallot in the peanut oil over a low to medium heat, stirring, for about 1 minute or so. Take care not to let the shallot mix brown or stick. Then add the slices of mango and turn in the spice mixture, adding the lemon juice and sugar. Use the water to moisten the mix if it looks too dry.

Cook over a low heat for about 10 minutes, until the mango is cooked and the syrup has combined to a moist, jammy consistency. It should not be too runny, or so solid that it sticks to the spoon!

FOR THE CHUTNEY

1 stick cinnamon

1 teaspoon hot Madras curry powder mix

2 whole cloves

1 small shallot, finely chopped

1 tablespoon peanut oil

4 large ripe mangoes, stoned, peeled and sliced

juice of 1 lemon

2 tablespoons palm sugar (soft brown Demerara will do)

4 tablespoons water

WARM SALAD OF
CHICKEN LIVERS
WITH A POACHED EGG

See photograph opposite page 48.

See photograph opposite page 48.

INGREDIENTS

450 g/1 lb smoked streaky bacon, rind removed and medium sliced

3 tablespoons olive oil

4 medium field mushrooms

675 g/1½ lb fresh chicken livers (duck livers are even better)

115 ml/4 fl oz mustard vinaigrette (made with whole-grain mustard and chopped spring onions)

8 eggs

mixed salad leaves, e.g. red Batavia, oak leaf or frisée

chopped parsley, to serve

This warm salad of chicken livers was a favourite in our old restaurant. It's light and yet a full-on salad at the same time. After all, salad is only salad — so you have got to do something to make it substantial — and this is it!

METHOD: Slice the bacon into 2.5-cm/1-in lardons, 5 mm/¼ in thick. Fry the bacon in half of the oil over a high flame until crispy, then remove from the frying pan with a slotted spoon and drain on kitchen paper. Slice the field mushrooms into 1-cm/½-in thick pieces and fry them lightly in the fat left in the pan for about 2 minutes. Remove from the pan and keep warm. These will be added to the pan when the livers are 'halfway done'.

Trim the chicken livers to clean them (if fresh livers are not available, then frozen ones will do but ensure that they are

NOSH TIP

Chicken livers are fragile and are best cooked by turning them over, when done on one side, with a palette knife. Resist the temptation to shake or jiggle the pan — the livers will break apart if handled roughly.

washed and drained dry — patting dry with tea towels is ideal). The best results are obtained if the livers are left whole and they are cooked at a hot temperature. Heat the remaining oil in the frying pan and, when smoking hot, fry the livers.

When the livers have been cooking for about 2 minutes or so each side (depending on size), add the bacon lardons and the warm mushroom slices. Shake a generous splash of the mustard vinaigrette into the pan to deglaze it, then remove from the heat. If your pan is small, you may have to cook the livers in two batches. Poach the eggs in just-boiling water with a dash of vinegar, no salt.

Divide the salad leaves between the serving plates. Spoon some livers and bacon and mushrooms over the leaves. Sprinkle the warm mustard dressing evenly over the salad. Using a slotted spoon, place a hot poached egg on top of each salad pile. Add some chopped parsley and serve immediately.

In Nosh philosophy, salad is a bit 'Nancy-Boy Potter food' so we've added some robust offal and meat to give it more substance!

SPICY PORK
WITH SPINACH

FOR THE GARLIC TOASTS

3 garlic cloves, peeled

3 tablespoons extra-virgin olive oil

8 thick slices ciabatta bread

FOR THE SPINACH WITH SAUSAGE

3 tablespoons olive oil

5 Italian pepper sausages, skins removed and meat crumbled

1.3 kg/3 lb baby spinach, washed and stalks removed

sea salt

3 tablespoons good-quality balsamic vinegar

Spinach, lightly wok-fried until wilted, makes a light but flavoursome starter, and is substantial enough for a quick meal. You will need a wok, preferably round-bottomed, set over a high gas flame to cook this dish. If you want to save time, you can pre-cook the sausage meat by stir-frying it around the pan for a few minutes, letting it cool, then covering with clingfilm and chilling until you're ready to cook later.

GARLIC TOASTS: Crush the garlic into the extra-virgin olive oil and paint it on to one side of the ciabatta slices. Grill under a hot flame to brown the bread and create garlic toasts.

SPINACH WITH SAUSAGE: Meanwhile, heat the wok all over the surface for some minutes until you see the metal go 'blue' (this shows you it is very hot). Then add half of the olive oil. (If you try to cook everything in one go, you'll end up cooling down the pan too much and stewing it, so cook in two or three lots.) When the oil is smoking hot, toss in the sausage meat and fry for a few minutes, until cooked. Drain off the excess oils. Throw in large bunches of spinach, tossing and turning it around the wok to wilt it. When all the greens have been incorporated, season with salt and deglaze with a few splashes of balsamic vinegar. The resulting mix can be placed over the hot garlic toasts and served immediately while still piping hot.

HOW TO SEASON YOUR WOK

A traditional steel wok has a light coating of machine oil from the factory to prevent it rusting. This has to be scrubbed off with steel wool and strong detergent. After rinsing thoroughly, heat the wok over a high flame until the metal 'blues' and discolours. Move the pan around the flame until the whole surface is discoloured and you are sure that all traces of any residual coating have been vapourized.

Next, allow the wok to cool somewhat so that a light coating of peanut or sunflower oil (or a similar oil) can be smeared over the new surface with kitchen paper. It also will tend to vapourize and give off smoke. The residue, however, will adhere to the pan and 'blacken it up'. Scrub the metal with ground salt and kitchen paper. Rinse with cold water. The wok is now seasoned. Do not, however, undo all your hard work by washing the wok in hot soapy water at any time. After cooking, just rinse out immediately with cold water (removing any stubborn bits with a steel wool scrubber). This will keep your wok in perfect condition.

As with all non-stick pans, even the best-quality Teflon surfaces wear and get scratched with time, so we would still recommend a traditional steel wok. Wooden-handled is best; metal ones are too hot to hold and thus difficult to manipulate.

GARLIC STUFFED
FIELD MUSHROOMS

2 garlic cloves, crushed

12 tablespoons olive oil

6 tablespoons fresh white breadcrumbs

2 tablespoons chopped flat-leaf parsley

6 large open field mushrooms

sea salt

freshly ground black pepper

This is a quick, easy and delicious way to start a meal — perfect for entertaining when you are in a rush with little time to cook but still want to serve up something special for your guests. You must use the large open cup field mushrooms (Agaricus campestris) for the best results.

METHOD: First, crush the garlic into the oil and then mix in the breadcrumbs and parsley. Spoon about 1 tablespoon of the garlic stuffing into each open mushroom 'cup' and season generously with salt and pepper.

Place the mushrooms in a grill pan and cook under a preheated hot grill. As the mushrooms are grilled, they will shrink slightly and some of the oil will leak out. Use this oil to baste the outside of each mushroom, creating a succulent result. About 5–10 minutes under the grill will suffice, depending on the temperature. Serve immediately.

HOT POTATO SALAD
WITH BACON AND EGG

This starter is so good that it's difficult to stop at just one portion! Again, it's another substantial salad which will appeal to everyone with a hearty appetite.

VINAIGRETTE: Dissolve the seasoning and sugar in the vinegars and then whisk in the oil, adding it gradually. Stir in the shallot and then set aside to rest for 30 minutes to let the flavours develop.

SALAD: Boil the potatoes in their skins until tender but still firm — they should be slightly waxy in the middle but not overcooked and falling apart. Drain and refresh in cold water. When lukewarm, skin them, dice into 1-cm/½-in chunks and set aside.

Pan-fry the bacon in the olive oil until well done, but not crispy. Drain on kitchen paper. Combine with the potatoes and spring onions. Peel the warm eggs and cut into large chunks. Add the eggs to the potato mixture with enough vinaigrette to 'bind' them together. Arrange the potato salad on a bed of salad leaves, sprinkle with chopped chives and, if liked, a few dashes of neat balsamic vinegar over the top.

FOR THE VINAIGRETTE

sea salt and freshly ground black pepper

1 teaspoon caster sugar

2 tablespoons red wine vinegar

1 tablespoon good quality aged balsamic vinegar

6 tablespoons virgin olive oil

1 shallot, finely chopped

FOR THE SALAD

900 g/2 lb waxy new potatoes

16 rashers smoked streaky bacon, chopped

2 tablespoons olive oil

1 bunch spring onions, trimmed and chopped

8 hard-boiled eggs, still warm

selection of mixed salad leaves

chopped chives, to serve

main
courses

ROAST BEEF WITH CELERIAC MASH

BEEF CASSEROLE WITH MUSHROOMS

STEAK AND KIDNEY PIE WITH GUINNESS

OXTAIL STEW WITH PORT

**SAUSAGES WITH APPLE
AND ONION MASH**

BRAISED LAMB NECK FILLET

PAN-FRIED BACON AND CALF'S LIVER

SPAGHETTI WITH PORK MEATBALLS

CASSOULET WITH TOULOUSE SAUSAGE

NOSH COQ AU VIN

**CHICKEN BIRIANI AND
MUSHROOM SAUCE**

**SMOKED HADDOCK KEDGEREE
WITH GINGER**

NOSH FISH PIE

MUSHROOM STUFFED RAVIOLI

**GRILLED DUCK BREAST
WITH FIG SAUCE**

SQUIDS STEWED IN INK

ROAST BEEF
WITH CELERIAC MASH

See photograph opposite page 49.

FOR THE BEEF

1 rib joint of British beef, about 5 ribs' width, about 6.75 kg/15 lb wet weight

4 tablespoons olive oil

sea salt and ground white pepper

1 large Spanish onion, thickly sliced

2 small carrots, thickly sliced

$^1/_2$ bottle robust red wine

NOSH TIP

For the meat to be well presented, it is important to allow the joint to rise to room temperature. This will take at least an hour from a standard fridge.

The great thing about the rib joint is that as the ribs diminish in size along the rack of ribs the meat emerges with differing degrees of rareness — the biggest end producing the rarest and the smaller end giving a more medium result. Thus all preferences are catered for. The celeriac and potato combo with vanilla makes an interesting departure from the traditional roast potatoes, but we give you our recipe for those as well, just in case. The creamed beetroot is spectacular with beef, and Yorkshire pudding is an unbeatable accompaniment. To complete the dish a green leafy vegetable is good; the crunchy texture of English cabbage will balance the celeriac and potato mash.

BEEF: Rub the surface of the joint with a little olive oil and sprinkle with white pepper and salt, rubbing it well into the crevices. Place in a roasting tin on top of the onion and carrots (which act as a trivet), and pour the red wine into the bottom of the tin. (You can drink the other half as you proceed further. It is a most enjoyable way to get the meal ready.)

Next, the meat must be roasted in a very hot preheated oven at 230°C/450°F/Gas Mark 8 for 20 minutes to seal it. Then, the temperature can be reduced to 200–220°C/400–425°F/Gas Mark 6–7 for the rest of the cooking time. If you allow 20 minutes per 450 g/1 lb, this should give you a rough guide, for a range from rare within the joint to medium/well done on the ends.

CELERIAC MASH: Meanwhile, cut the peeled celeriac and potatoes into chunks. Cook until tender in enough chicken stock to cover them. Drain and mouli the mash together in the usual way, then add the olive oil (instead of the more usual butter), adjusting the seasoning as necessary. When combined, add the vanilla essence and stir well. Set aside to await the meat.

To reheat, simply stir around slowly over a low flame, ensuring that the mixture does not catch and stick. Before serving, check the vanilla flavour. Vanilla is a volatile essence and may lose some of its potency while standing, so add more, if necessary. If using vanilla essence in the celeriac mash (which is stronger) reduce to 2 teaspoonsful.

SERVING THE MEAT: When the meat is ready (a judicious prod of the end surfaces will show how well-done it is, and a meat thermometer is also a useful guide), take it out to rest under a sheet of kitchen foil for at least 15 minutes. This will give you time to prepare the gravy and allow the fibres of the beef to loosen and become set for carving. Carving should be done onto warm plates, the rarest slices coming from the middle of the large end.

GRAVY: This is easily made by reducing the meat juices and wine on the top of the hob, then straining them through a fine wire sieve, and adjusting for seasoning. Add a little celeriac water to give a savoury addition (not too much as the celery taste must not dominate the meaty flavours). It is important, too, not to have added a lot of salt to the original meat surface — remember, reduction increases all the flavours, including salt, so don't overdo it.

FOR THE CELERIAC MASH

3 large heads celeriac, peeled

1.4 kg/3 lb potatoes (Maris Piper), peeled

light chicken stock

175–225 ml/6–8 fl oz extra-virgin olive oil

freshly ground black pepper/horseradish sauce

2 tablespoons fresh vanilla extract (Madagascan is good), to taste

---

IMPORTANT

A rib of beef this size is about the biggest object you'll probably ever put in your conventional or convecting oven. Halfway through the cooking time, rotate the meat so that the heat absorbed will be even. Fan ovens are supposed to roast evenly, but huge pieces of beef impede air flow around the oven — so be warned.

ROAST BEEF WITH
CELERIAC MASH *continued*

YORKSHIRE PUDDING

115 g/4 oz plain flour

a large pinch of salt

300 ml/1/2 pint whole milk

1 large egg (or 2 small), lightly beaten

1 tablespoon melted butter

4 tablespoons melted beef dripping

NOSH TIP

Batter poured into hot beef dripping will produce the best results. If poured into a cold or lukewarm tin, the Yorkshire will never rise properly. The depth of the batter in the tray should be no more than 1 cm/1/2 in.

YORKSHIRE PUDDING: Sift the flour and salt into a mixing bowl and beat to a smooth texture with half of the milk plus the beaten egg(s) and the melted butter. Stir in the remaining milk, and whisk together well. Leave for 15 minutes to allow the glutens to emerge. This will ensure a better result.

About 35 minutes before the meat is to be taken out, place the beef dripping in the oven in a large 25–30 cm/10–12 in baking tray. Allow to heat through for 4–5 minutes, until smoking, and then pour in the batter. Place in the top of the oven for 10–15 minutes, then on the bottom for another 15 minutes. Finally, when the meat is removed, place the tin in the middle to finish and crisp up around the edges. The initial heat raises the batter, the bottom cooking cooks it right through, and the final browning avoids a soggy middle. Good luck, and remember, a hot start is the key to success.

CREAMED BEETROOT

This makes a great-tasting accompaniment — perfect with all beef dishes. Coarsely grate cooked whole beetroots into a béchamel sauce made with single cream instead of milk — enough sauce to coat the beetroot. Add a dash of lemon juice and plenty of freshly ground black pepper and stir slowly in a saucepan to reheat.

ROAST POTATOES: Some people cook their potatoes from raw, and some parboil them. If parboiled, they cook quicker and, being floury in texture, they absorb more of the roasting fat and get a better, crisper result.

Peel and boil the potatoes whole for about 10 minutes, depending on their size, and refresh in cold water. The potatoes should then be sprinkled liberally with sea salt and black pepper. Heat the goose fat or beef dripping until smoking hot in a roasting tray and then pile the spuds into the tray, taking care not to splash the fat around. Place in the oven towards the latter half of the meat cooking time, until they are brown and crisp.

SAVOY CABBAGE: Trim off any yellowed or torn bits from the cabbage but try to retain as many as possible of the outer leaves, as the dark green parts have much of the strong flavour needed here. Slice the cabbage in two, remove the tough stalk at the base and slice the leaves into 1-cm/^{1}/$_2$-in wide strips across the grain of the layers.

Sauté the garlic in the butter for a couple of minutes over a low heat without letting it brown, and then add the cabbage, turning it regularly for another 3–4 minutes. Add half of the hot stock and the nutmeg, put a lid on the pot, and braise for another 5 minutes or so, turning occasionally.

Like pasta, the cabbage should be slightly *al dente* with a moist coating of the reduced juices. If needed, add more stock to the cabbage, but don't drown it — the residue should just cover and cling to the cabbage, the butter giving it a good shine. If necessary, season only lightly.

ROAST POTATOES

2.25 kg/5 lb old potatoes

sea salt and freshly ground black pepper

3 tablespoons goose fat or beef dripping

SAVOY CABBAGE

1 large Savoy cabbage

1 garlic clove, crushed

50 g/2 oz unsalted butter

300 ml/^{1}/$_2$ pint hot light chicken stock

a large pinch of freshly grated nutmeg

salt and ground white pepper

BEEF CASSEROLE
WITH MUSHROOMS

INGREDIENTS

6 rashers smoked streaky bacon, rind removed

5 tablespoons olive oil

2 large Spanish onions, finely chopped

1 tablespoon brown sugar

450 g/1 lb small shallots, peeled, left whole

1.8 kg/4 lb shin of beef (untrimmed weight)

3 tablespoons plain flour

sea salt and ground white pepper

225 g/8 oz small button mushrooms, washed and halved

2 garlic cloves, crushed

1 bottle robust red wine, e.g. Rioja

1 bouquet garni (bay, rosemary, thyme, etc.)

zest and juice of 1 small orange

300 ml/1/2 pint beef stock

freshly ground black pepper

freshly chopped parsley, to serve

Cheaper cuts of beef, like the shin used here, benefit from slow, even cooking. The mistake some people make is to buy very lean-looking cuts (which appeal to the eye on the supermarket shelf, but don't have enough fat marbled throughout) and then cut the meat into pieces that are too small. On cooking, this has the effect of drying out the flesh and giving a stringy unappealing result. Resist the supermarkets' trim packaging and get some well-marbled meat.

CASSEROLE: Trim the large edge of bacon fat off the rashers. Chop this into small dice and fry slowly over a low heat in 2 tablespoons of the oil until the fat releases its juices and is rendered down. Then add the onions, raise the heat to medium and continue cooking for about 5 minutes, adding the sugar, until the onions are browned. Don't worry about overdoing the onions — a small amount of slightly 'burnt' edges on them lends itself quite well to this particular dish. Remove the onions and reserve.

Now slice the bacon into narrow strips and pan-fry until well done, then remove with a slotted spoon and reserve with the onions. Add the remaining oil to the pan and brown the whole shallots over a high heat until they are coloured dark brown, but are not cooked through. Drain, remove and reserve.

Next, trim the beef, removing any sinewy membranes, and cut into large steak-size pieces. Lightly coat the beef pieces with lightly seasoned flour, shaking off any excess. Changing the heat to a high flame, brown a couple of pieces of beef at a time.

Cook the mushrooms briefly with the garlic, and reserve. Now, deglaze any residues left in the pan with a couple of dashes of the red wine. Fill a casserole with layers of onion, bacon, meat, mushrooms, the remainder of the wine, the bouquet garni, orange juice and zest and the stock. Put a lid (or foil) over the top and cook in a medium-hot preheated oven at 180°C/350°F/Gas Mark 4 for about an hour, and then arrange the reserved shallots over the top. Cook for a further 1–1¹/₂ hours, until the meat is soft, but not falling apart.

Drain the juices off (discarding the bouquet garni) and reduce in a saucepan at a rolling boil by about half to two-thirds their original volume, until the reduction has a dense consistency. Adjust the seasoning if necessary, adding freshly ground black pepper, and return the juices to the casserole. This dish is finished off with a sprinkling of freshly chopped parsley.

BEEF STOCK: Brown the beef and veal bones and trimmings in a hot oven at 220°C/425°F/Gas Mark 7 for 15–20 minutes, then place in a large stockpot with all the ingredients down to and including the white wine, and bring to the boil. Boil until the wine has nearly evaporated and then add the cold water. Add the herbs, bouquet garni and spices, and bring to the boil. Simmer for 4 hours, skimming the surface frequently. When cooked, strain through a fine conical strainer. Now place over a high heat to boil and reduce the stock by at least half its volume. Resting the liquid in the fridge for a couple of hours when cooled ensures that any fat congeals on the top and can be removed easily.

FOR THE BEEF STOCK

1.1 kg/2¹/₂ lb broken beef bones and trimmings

450 g/1 lb veal bones and trimmings

50 g/2 oz streaky bacon, chopped

1 tablespoon tomato purée

115 g/4 oz carrots, finely diced

115 g/4 oz mushrooms, finely diced

115 g/4 oz onion, peeled and finely diced

115 g/4 oz leek, finely diced

2 fresh tomatoes, deseeded and skinned

1 shallot, chopped

2 garlic cloves, crushed

600 ml/1 pint white wine

2.3 litres/4 pints cold water

a bunch of parsley stalks

a pinch each of dried tarragon and chervil

1 bouquet garni (thyme, parsley, bay, etc.)

6 black peppercorns

1 clove

STEAK AND KIDNEY
PIE WITH GUINNESS

1.3 kg/3 lb stewing beef (shin is good)

450 g/1 lb veal or ox kidney

4 tablespoons olive oil

1 tablespoon unsalted butter

2 Spanish onions, thinly sliced

1 teaspoon caster sugar

600 ml/1 pint beef stock

300 ml/¹/₂ pint draught Guinness

pinch of dried thyme

1 tablespoon Worcestershire sauce

25 g/1 oz plain flour

sea salt and white pepper

2 large blocks rough puff pastry, preferably fresh

eggwash, for brushing

This dish probably typifies the best in traditional English cooking. Meaty, robust and strong flavoured, it is a pub lunch favourite and has a strong memorable appeal when we want 'comforting food'.

METHOD: Trim all the excess fat from the meat and cut into largish cubes, about 2.5 cm/1 in square. Trim the kidneys of any sinewy threads and slice into 5-mm/¹/₄-in pieces.

Heat the oil and butter in a large flameproof casserole (supplied with a lid) and fry the onions with the sugar and butter over a very high heat until they turn dark brown. Add the meat and 'seal off' the steak and kidney pieces. Season only lightly at this stage as the liquids will be reduced later. If some onion edges subsequently have an almost burnt edge to them, don't worry — in this case, they will add flavour to the final dish.

Add the beef stock and Guinness and scrape up any sediment from the bottom of the casserole. Add a pinch of thyme and the Worcestershire sauce, and bring to the boil. Then cover

the casserole with a lid and reduce the heat to a slow simmer.
Cook gently for about 2 hours, until the meat is really tender.

Before decanting into a pie dish, it is important for the
sauce to be thick and gooey. This is easily done by removing
the meat and bubbling and reducing the liquids on a hot
hob until the sauce is dense and syrupy. The gravy can be
thickened finally by stirring in some flour, mixed with a little
cold water to prevent lumps, a spoonful at a time. The resulting
gravy can then be checked for seasoning and recombined with
the cooked meat.

Put the meat and gravy mixture into 2 pie dishes or a large
lasagne-type dish. Roll out the puff pastry, 2.5 mm/$^1/_8$ in thick, and
lay over the top of the pie filling. You can wet the edge of the
dish with eggwash to prevent the gravy leaking and bubbling out
during cooking. Poke a thin cut with a sharp knife into the middle
of the pastry lid to let the steam escape.

Bake the pie in the middle of a preheated hot oven at
200°C/400°F/Gas Mark 6 for 30 minutes or so, until the crust has
risen and is crisp and golden brown. This dish is best enjoyed hot.

OXTAIL STEW
WITH PORT

4 oxtails cut from the middle, fat trimmed

3 tablespoons seasoned flour

50 ml/2 fl oz olive oil

675 g/1½ lb carrots, cut into large chunks

115 g/4 oz leeks, finely chopped

225 g/8 oz Spanish onions, sliced

150 ml/¼ pint robust red wine

600 ml/1 pint beef stock

1 tablespoon orange juice

300 ml/½ pint port

1 tablespoon fresh thyme

2 bay leaves

2 cloves

1 teaspoon caster sugar

2 garlic cloves, peeled

1 tablespoon tomato purée

1 marrow bone 'core' (see note)

salt and ground black pepper

3 tablespoons fresh chopped parsley

The meat nearest the bone is often the sweetest and oxtail looks, at first sight, nearly all bone. However, when slowly cooked to perfection, the meat melts away and produces a gelatinous rich gravy that is hard to beat.

METHOD: This tends to be quite a fatty dish so ensure that the oxtail bones are well trimmed of any fat around the outside. Dust them with lightly seasoned flour (see tip) and then brown in the hot oil in a frying pan. When browned, remove and drain and transfer to a deep-sided, heavy-based casserole dish with a lid.

In the remaining oil in the pan, fry the carrots, leeks and onions for 5–10 minutes over medium heat, taking care to turn them occasionally to prevent them sticking and burning. Then decant the vegetables into the casserole pot and place it over the heat.

Now add the red wine and allow the alcohol to 'boil off' for a few minutes. Add the beef stock, orange juice and port. Tip in the herbs, cloves, sugar and garlic, and bring to the boil. Then replace the

MARROW BONE CORE

Ask your butcher to split a marrow bone for you so that you can scrape out the jelly 'core' in the centre of the bone.

lid, turn down the heat very low and simmer for 2 hours, stirring occasionally to turn the meats over in the cooking liquid.

Remove the casserole from the heat and allow the stew to cool until the fat solidifies on the surface, where it can be skimmed off and discarded.

Then bring the stew back to the boil, add the tomato purée and the marrow bone jelly. Cover the casserole and cook in a preheated low oven at 150°C/300°F/Gas Mark 2 for 2¹/₂–3 hours, until the meat is almost coming away from the bone.

Adjust the seasoning to taste — it is important to season mainly at the end of cooking as too much reduction of the juices will result in too salty a taste if the seasoning is overdone at the start. Serve the stew sprinkled with chopped parsley. If the stew liquid looks too thin, just decant it into a clean pan and a quick bubble on the hob will reduce it.

NOSH TIP

To season flour, just add a little sea salt and some white or black pepper to plain flour and mix together.

" This has to be one of the richest dishes on the planet — and it's well worth the effort. "

SAUSAGES WITH APPLE AND ONION MASH

FOR THE SAUSAGES

16 large wild boar sausages

4 tablespoons olive oil

sea salt and white pepper

FOR THE APPLE AND ONION MASH

1.8 kg/4 lb 'old' potatoes, cut into even-sized pieces

2 large Spanish onions, sliced

4 tablespoons olive oil

12 tablespoons Bramley apple purée

sea salt and freshly ground black pepper

50 g/2 oz slightly salted butter

Everyone loves sausages — they're almost a national dish. The gamey taste of wild boar makes them a gourmet delight, and the apple sauce in the potato complements this exactly.

SAUSAGES: The sausages can be either pan-fried to colour them up and then roasted in the oven, or they can be lightly oiled with 2 tablespoons of the olive oil, seasoned and grilled under a hot grill. As the sausages are quite coarse, traditionally, we prefer to pan-fry them and then put the frying pan (no wood or plastic handles) in a hot oven at 230°C/450°F/Gas Mark 8 for 15 minutes, turning them once.

APPLE AND ONION MASH: Boil the potatoes in salted water until tender and meanwhile fry the sliced onions in the olive oil for about 10 minutes, stirring occasionally, until browned and thoroughly cooked. Drain the potatoes and mash in the pan. A mouli is good for this. Over very gentle heat, stir into the mashed potato the apple purée and half of the fried onions and then season with salt and pepper. Add the knob of butter and stir in.

Serve the grilled wild boar sausages on top of the apple and onion mash with the remaining half of the fried onions.

Opposite: Warm salad of chicken livers with a poached egg (page 30).

BRAISED LAMB
NECK FILLET

For this recipe, make a stock as per the chicken stock method (see page 19) and add the lamb neck bones with a sprig of rosemary. Simmer for 1 hour, skimming off any scum. Strain, pass through a fine sieve and boil to reduce to a strongly flavoured stock.

METHOD: Shell and cook the peas for 7–10 minutes in boiling water to which a chicken stock cube has been added. Drain and purée through the coarse mesh sieve of a mouli, then stir in 25 g/1 oz of the butter and season to taste. Keep warm. Trim all the fat and sinews off the lamb fillets and season them. Seal them off in the olive oil in a heavy-based casserole dish, turning them in the oil until they start to brown on all sides. Remove and set aside.

Reserve the juices and turn down the heat to low–medium, then add the remaining butter with the rosemary and shallots. Cook gently for 5 minutes, until softened. Discard the rosemary and add the red wine. Return the lamb fillets to the casserole with the reserved juices and reduced lamb stock. Cover with a lid and cook in a preheated oven at 180°C/350°F/Gas Mark 4 for 30–40 minutes. Cook the spinach in a wok over high heat. Sprinkle with a little butter and salt, season with nutmeg and then arrange on the serving plates to form a bed for the lamb.

To serve, cut each fillet into thick slices and place a portion on each spinach bed. Serve with the peas and gravy.

Opposite: Roast beef with celeriac mash (page 38).

INGREDIENTS

900 g/2 lb fresh peas in their pods

1 chicken stock cube

50 g/2 oz butter

4 large neck fillets, with bones

sea salt and ground white pepper

3 tablespoons olive oil

1 sprig fresh rosemary

6 shallots, finely chopped

1 glass of red wine

600 ml/1 pint lamb stock (see introduction)

1.3 kg/3 lb baby spinach, washed

1/2 teaspoon grated nutmeg

freshly ground black pepper

NOSH TIP

A quick 'bubble' on the hob will reduce and thicken the gravy.

PAN-FRIED BACON AND
CALF'S LIVER

INGREDIENTS

8 x 175-g/6-oz portions of best quality calf's liver, trimmed and sliced 1 cm/¹/₂ in thick

1 tablespoon balsamic vinegar

sea salt and ground white pepper

3 tablespoons olive oil

8 rashers dry-cured back bacon or pancetta

2 large Spanish onions, thinly sliced

2 garlic cloves, peeled

6 tablespoons veal (or beef) stock

mashed potato, to serve

freshly ground black pepper

This dish requires the very best calf's liver. Dutch and French traditional farming methods use a milk-fed diet for the beasts and this gives the best results.

METHOD: Clean each slice of liver to ensure that the 'tubes' of connective tissue are trimmed away. 'Wet' each slice of liver with a little balsamic vinegar and season with salt and a sprinkling of white pepper.

Heat the olive oil in a frying pan over high heat and fry each rasher of bacon or pancetta until moderately well-done — the fat that is rendered down will remain in the pan to cook the liver. Remove the bacon, drain on kitchen paper and keep warm. Sauté the onions until golden brown, reducing the heat to medium after a couple of minutes to prevent the onions burning. You want them to cook gradually to bring out the sweetness in

NOSH TIP

Fresh calf's liver shrinks dramatically when first pan-fried, so ensure that you don't cut it too thin to start with. Chilling the liver slices well beforehand keeps them from breaking apart in the pan — calf's liver is quite fragile.

them. When they are well-coloured up, remove them from the pan and keep warm.

Finally, adding a little more oil if the pan looks too dry, sauté the slices of liver, one at a time, with the garlic cloves, until the liver is medium-rare. It should be cooked through but still retain a reasonable degree of pinkness in the centre. Watch carefully, as overcooked liver is dry and useless, whereas if it is too rare, it will not have a 'bite' to it. When the liver is almost done, discard the garlic cloves and add some onions to the few dashes of veal stock. At this point, you could add a dash of red wine, if wished, but as the liver has been marinated in balsamic vinegar, this may be 'gilding the lily'!

To serve, arrange the slices of liver and the onions over some simple mashed potato with the bacon, and pour some rich pan gravy around it. Sprinkle with a grinding of black pepper.

> *If you can't afford calf's liver, lamb's liver will make a reasonably good substitute. However, avoid pig's liver which has a slightly bitter flavour.*

SPAGHETTI
WITH PORK MEATBALLS

FOR THE MEATBALLS

800 g/1 3/4 lb lean pork mince

2 medium Spanish onions, finely chopped

1 teaspoon dried oregano

3 garlic cloves, pulped

4 tablespoons finely grated Parmesan

1/2 teaspoon ground nutmeg

1 egg, beaten

2 tablespoons olive oil

FOR THE SPAGHETTI SAUCE

2 glasses white wine

1.2 litres/2 pints tomato sauce (see opposite)

1 teaspoon dried oregano

1 clove

25 g/1 oz unsalted butter

900 g/2 lb spaghetti

shaved Parmesan, to serve

freshly ground black pepper

P ork mince is used for this dish. Although it is often seen on the supermarket shelf, you may be unsure of what to do with it. Here's an excellent variation on an Italian theme.

MEATBALLS: Combine the pork mince with the onions, oregano, garlic, Parmesan and nutmeg. Mix in the beaten egg to bind the mixture together. Shape into small walnut-sized balls, then chill in the fridge for 1 hour to help them keep their shape. Heat the olive oil in a high-sided casserole dish over a hot flame and seal and lightly brown each meatball. Take care not to overdo the sealing process or the meatballs will dry out. When all the meatballs have been sealed off, remove them with a slotted spoon.

SPAGHETTI SAUCE: Deglaze the casserole dish with the white wine and allow to bubble for a minute. Then add the tomato and basil sauce, oregano and clove. Bring to the boil, reduce the heat, add the meatballs and cover the pan. Simmer for about 30 minutes, until the meatballs are cooked through. Finally, add a small lump of butter, and stir it through to give the sauce a shine.

While the sauce is cooking, cook the spaghetti in a large pan of boiling lightly salted water until it is just tender but still retains some 'bite' (*al dente*). Drain well and toss some of the sauce through the pasta. It should not be runny but should cling to the strands.

Serve immediately with more meatballs and sauce spooned on top of the spaghetti, with some shaved Parmesan and a good grinding of black pepper.

TOMATO SAUCE: Pass the tomatoes through a fine mouli sieve to remove the seeds and skin. Heat the olive oil in a solid-based saucepan over a medium heat and add the onion, garlic, basil, oregano and white pepper. Stir briskly to prevent the onion browning. When the onion has softened, add the tomato pulp and basil. Bring the mixture to the boil and immediately reduce the heat to a low simmer. Remove the garlic and discard.

Stir in the sugar (this balances the acidity of the tomatoes) and half of the salt. Simmer the sauce for about 30 minutes, until well reduced. The solids will tend to condense on the bottom of the pan, so stir with a wooden spoon occasionally. The time taken will vary, depending on the degree of wateriness of the original canned tomato contents, so keep an eye on the pan. Remove the basil stalks before serving. Season the finished sauce with freshly ground black pepper.

FOR THE TOMATO SAUCE

2 x 400-g/14-oz cans Italian plum tomatoes with their juices

50 ml/2 fl oz olive oil

^{1}/$_2$ medium Spanish onion, finely chopped

2 large garlic cloves

^{1}/$_2$ small bunch fresh sweet basil, about 12 g/^{1}/$_2$ oz

^{1}/$_2$ tablespoon fresh or dried oregano

pinch of ground white pepper

1 teaspoon caster sugar

^{1}/$_2$ teaspoon sea salt

freshly ground black pepper

CASSOULET WITH
TOULOUSE SAUSAGE

675 g/1¹/₂ lb fresh white haricot beans, soaked overnight in water, then drained (or 5 x 400-g/14-oz cans, drained)

350 g/12 oz salted pork belly or ribs, soaked overnight in water

225 g/8 oz fresh pork rind, tied in a bundle and parboiled for 1 minute

3 carrots, peeled whole

450 g/1 lb very ripe tomatoes, peeled, deseeded and diced

2 onions, stuck with 2 cloves

sea salt and pepper

2 medium tomatoes, peeled and chopped

1 bouquet garni ('teabag' type is OK)

This is a typical peasant dish from the Languedoc area of France. It is very substantial and the quantities given here will feed ten hungry people.

BEANPOT: Put the drained haricot beans and all the other ingredients for the beanpot in a large, heavy pot, cover with plenty of water and simmer over a low heat for about 2 hours, until the beans and vegetables are tender. If you are using canned beans, you can reduce the cooking time to 45 minutes.

SAUTÉ: Brown the lamb in the goose fat. Add the chopped onions and garlic and brown lightly. Spoon over enough liquid from the bean pot to barely cover the meat, then add the tomatoes, seasoning and bouquet garni and simmer for 1¹/₂ hours. Brown the sausage and drumsticks in the bacon fat and add to the pot, then simmer for another 10 minutes.

Preheat the oven to 180°C/350°F/Gas Mark 4. Remove the bouquet garni, whole carrots and onion from the beanpot and discard. Remove the meat and pork rind and cut into large chunks. Rub inside a clean ovenproof pot with a cut garlic clove and place half of the beanpot mixture inside, add all of the meat and cover with the remaining beanpot mixture.

Bring back to the boil on the top of the stove, sprinkle with breadcrumbs and then bake in the oven for 1¹/₂ hours, breaking any 'crust' that forms and stirring it into the cassoulet. Repeat every 15 minutes or so until you have stirred in 4-5 crusts and leave the last crust to brown before serving.

FOR THE SAUTÉ

450 g/1 lb boneless shoulder of lamb, cut into chunks

1 tablespoonful goose fat

2 onions, chopped

3 garlic cloves, chopped

2 tomatoes, deseeded and chopped

salt and pepper

1 bouquet garni

20-cm/8-in piece of Toulouse-type sausage

2 duck, goose or chicken drumsticks

1 tablespoon bacon fat

50 g/2 oz dried breadcrumbs

NOSH TIP

This dish takes some while to make but, once made, can be easily reheated to serve over a period and is very substantial and 'warming'.

NOSH
COQ AU VIN

See photograph opposite page 65.

See photograph opposite page 65.

INGREDIENTS

I large 2.7 kg/6 lb roasting
chicken (premier quality)

4 tablespoons olive oil

225 g/8 oz smoked streaky
bacon, cut into large lardons

225 g/8 oz baby onions, peeled

2 carrots

2 leeks, cleaned, green tops
(flags) intact

2 sticks celery, peeled and diced

4 whole garlic cloves, peeled

4 shallots, peeled and sliced

115 g/4 oz closed cup mushrooms

3 bay leaves

small handful of chopped oregano/
thyme (or 2 teaspoons each dried)

juice and zest of I orange

1/2 bottle red wine

600 ml/I pint chicken stock

dash of Cognac

3 tablespoons chopped parsley

sea salt and ground black pepper

This is a classic French dish that had its heyday in the hip Sixties dinner party. Now it has more or less passed into cooking history. The only reservation we had about this, in principle, was that the wine gravy was always a bit thin. We have rectified this by reducing the juices accordingly. The best results are obtained by using good-quality ingredients. Try to get a free-range or first division bird — cheap old battery chook will not have much flavour.

METHOD: Joint the chicken into smallish pieces — the 'backbone' section and any other 'bony' bits, e.g. the neck, giblets, etc., can be cooked whole for flavour, and removed at the last stage when the stock is reduced.

Brown the chicken pieces all over in the olive oil in a hot frying pan. Decant the chicken into a large heavy-based casserole pot with a lid. In the remaining oil, brown the bacon lardons and then transfer them to the casserole. Next, brown the baby onions over a high heat, shaking and moving them in the pan until they are well-browned all over. Then decant them into a separate bowl and reserve until later. If added to the casserole at this early stage, they will become overcooked and break apart, losing their distinctive round character.

Finally, turn the heat down to medium and sweat off the remaining vegetables for 5–10 minutes, until they start to colour up. Add them to the casserole pot with the herbs, orange juice and zest, wine and chicken stock.

Cook in a medium-hot preheated oven at 190°C/ 375°F/ Gas Mark 5 for about 1 hour, or until the meat is starting to melt off the bone. Take out any unwanted pieces, such as the backbone section, neck, giblets and bay leaves, and discard them. Add the reserved baby onions to the casserole pot and cook for a further 30 minutes.

Pour off the juices and liquid into a clean pan and boil until they reduce enough to coat the back of a spoon. Return them to the chicken and vegetable mixture. Add a dash of Cognac, season to taste with salt and freshly ground black pepper, and sprinkle with a handful of freshly chopped parsley. Covered, the Coq au Vin will keep warm for at least 15 minutes.

This goes well with almost any vegetables you care to serve as an accompaniment. Favourites with us are floury potatoes, boiled whole and then mashed into the rich gravy with your fork.

> *This is such a fine dish that we suspect the French stole it from the English repertoire years ago and changed its name. We've reclaimed it!*

CHICKEN BIRIANI
AND MUSHROOM SAUCE

FOR THE RICE

FOR THE RICE

450 g/1 lb Basmati rice

1 x 1.8 kg/4 lb roasting chicken

**6 tablespoons peanut or
sunflower oil**

75 g/3 oz unsalted butter

3 large red onions, finely chopped

4 garlic cloves, crushed

**1 green pepper, cored, deseeded
and chopped small**

**4 small green chillies, deseeded
and finely sliced**

1 teaspoon Madras curry powder

6 small pieces of cinnamon bark

3 cloves

2 tablespoons whole cumin seeds

3 or 4 cardamon pods, crushed

600 ml/1 pint chicken stock

juice of 1 lemon

sea salt and white pepper

1/2 teaspoon saffron strands

1 teaspoon Garam Masala

**4 large tomatoes, each cut into 6
wedges**

I ndian food is a favourite with most people and here is a warming winter dish that goes a long way — typical of a traditional Indian meal.

RICE: Wash the rice in fresh cold water, rinsing and discarding the water about 10 times until the rinsing water runs fairly clear. Then drain and cover the rice with boiling water for 5 minutes. This allows some moisture to enter the grains. Meanwhile, joint and skin the chicken, removing all the bones, and cut up the meat into small 1-cm/1/2-in cubes.

Heat the oil in a large saucepan with a tightly fitting lid to a medium/medium-hot temperature. Add the butter and fry the onions, garlic, pepper, chillies, spices (except the Garam Masala, which will be added later) and chicken for about 5 minutes, uncovered, until the chicken has been 'sealed off'.

Drain the rice and add to the chicken and spice mixture. Fry, stirring continuously, for 2 or 3 minutes. Then add the chicken stock and lemon juice, season, bring to the boil and stir. Lower the heat to a slow simmer and cook with the lid on the pan.

After 5 minutes or so, uncover the biriani and sprinkle the saffron in a small pile on top of the rice on one 'edge' of the pan. Flick some rice grains on top of the saffron, moisten with a teaspoonful of water and cover the pan. This will colour and flavour the small area of rice a bright yellow/red colour, which is distinctive of saffron, and which can then be stirred-through the mixture prior to serving. This distributes the saffron rice randomly through the mixture and gives a pukka effect.

The rice should take another 10 minutes or so to cook (less time than is normal due to the previous 'soaking time') and the final mixture can be stirred through, adding the Garam Masala and the tomatoes. But do not overcook the rice. The biriani, when ready, should be moist but fluffy and light — somewhere between a Chinese-style fried rice and an Italian-style risotto but not quite as 'wet'.

SAUCE: Fry the onions, pepper, curry leaves, chillies, garlic, ginger, spices and seeds in the medium-hot oil, stirring occasionally, for about 3–5 minutes, until the onions and pepper are soft. Add the mushrooms and stir around so that they cook evenly and release their 'juices' into the sauce. Add the tomatoes, mix through and cook for another 5 minutes. You may need to add some water, in small dashes, to keep the sauce from drying out — cover the pan at this stage and keep an eye on it. The consistency of the final sauce should be quite wet and should be able to be poured on top of the biriani. Crisp, fried poppadums go well with this dish.

MUSHROOM SAUCE

2 large red onions, finely chopped

1 red pepper, deseeded and chopped

8 curry leaves

2 small red or green chillies, deseeded and finely chopped

4 garlic cloves, finely crushed

1 small 2.5-cm/1-in piece root ginger, peeled and finely grated

1 tablespoon Madras curry powder

1 tablespoon Garam Masala

1 teaspoon cumin seeds

1 teaspoon fenugreek seeds

4 tablespoons peanut or sunflower oil for frying

450 g/1 lb button (closed cup) mushrooms, rinsed and chopped or quartered

4 tomatoes, finely chopped

6 tablespoons water

NOSH TIP

Warn your guests that they will find seeds, bark, etc. throughout the dish, but don't take any stick for this if you get any whingers.

SMOKED HADDOCK
KEDGEREE WITH GINGER

INGREDIENTS

450 g/1 lb Basmati rice

1 teaspoon salt

675 g/1 1/2 lb smoked haddock

2 Spanish onions, finely chopped

50 g/2 oz unsalted butter

1 teaspoon Madras curry powder

1 teaspoon Garam Masala

2 pieces cinnamon stick

25-g/1-oz piece of fresh root ginger, peeled and finely chopped

75 ml/3 fl oz milk

pinch of saffron

300 ml/1/2 pint single cream

1 generous handful of chopped parsley and coriander, mixed

6 eggs, hard-boiled and cut into quarters

sea salt and ground white pepper

We experimented with several versions of this traditional English brunch dish to get some added zing to it. The fresh ginger got the vote. This dish has a special place in our repertoire as it was brought back from India by a relative, Viscount Edward Nosh.

METHOD: Prepare the rice by washing it in cold water about 6 times, or until the water runs clear, to remove the starch. Cook by adding one-and-a-half times the volume of the rice as cold water and bringing to the boil in a saucepan with a tightly fitting lid. When the water just boils, add 1 teaspoon salt, stir the rice once only, place a lid on the saucepan and simmer over a very low heat for about 10 minutes. Test the rice by sampling a few grains — it should be soft but not mushy. If it's still a little hard, add a dash of boiling water from a kettle. Fork through once and then leave to rest with the lid on.

NOSH TIP

Kedgeree should have a moist consistency and should not be 'dry'. Washing the rice until the water runs clear will ensure a non-sticky result. It is perfect traditionally for a brunch but it also serves well as a light dinner dish.

While the rice is cooking, skin and debone the haddock and fry the chopped onions in the butter until soft, adding the spices and ginger. When the onions are done, place the fish in the pan and add the milk and saffron. Lightly poach the fish for a few minutes over a low heat. When the fish is cooked, flake the flesh into large pieces into the frying pan and add the single cream. Stir around gently to mix the ingredients, add the parsley and coriander and mix into the cooked rice with the quartered eggs. Season with salt and ground white pepper.

" *This dish was stolen by a clever Englishman, our relative Viscount Edward Nosh, who loved his 'kitchri' at Lahore so much that he kidnapped his cook, forcing him at bayonet point to reveal the secrets of the recipe.* "

NOSH **FISH PIE**

See photograph opposite page 64.

See photograph opposite page 64.

FOR THE FISH PIE

900 g/2 lb white fish (haddock is good)

1.3 litres/2¼ pints milk

1 onion, chopped

2 bay leaves

a few peppercorns

pinch of grated nutmeg

2 cloves

225 g/8 oz fresh white breadcrumbs

12 plum (or tasty vine) tomatoes, skinned

sea salt and freshly ground black pepper

175 g/6 oz mature Cheddar, grated

50 g/2 oz unsalted butter, chilled and diced

finely chopped parsley, to serve

Despite its nursery associations, this is a supper dish that really warrants adult attention. By using top-quality fish, you can give it a classy feel. We are indebted to Mother N. Nosh for this fish pie recipe. Unlike most traditional recipes, which use a flaky pastry lid or mashed potato or similar, this has a cheese sauce and a gratin of breadcrumbs to complete the dish. Brother Nick owes his robust frame to such stout and honest fare.

FISH PIE: Lightly poach the fish in the milk with the onion, bay leaves, peppercorns, nutmeg and cloves. Cook gently over a low heat, until the fish is tender and starts to flake. Remove it from the poaching liquid with a slotted spoon and set aside. Leave the flavoured milk to infuse and rest for 20 minutes, then strain. You will need this milk to make the cheese sauce.

Grease a large pie dish with some butter — an oval gratin dish or lasagne-type dish are best. Sprinkle with a thick layer of the breadcrumbs, reserving the rest. Cut the tomatoes into 5-mm/¼-in thick slices and arrange a layer over the base of the dish. Season with salt and pepper.

Remove the skin and any bones from the poached fish and flake it lightly. Sprinkle half of the flaked fish over the tomatoes in the dish. Cover with half of the cheese sauce, and then repeat the layering, finishing with a layer of cheese sauce on top. Sprinkle with grated Cheddar, then the remaining breadcrumbs, and, finally, dot with little knobs of butter.

Bake the fish pie in a preheated oven at 170°C/325°F/Gas Mark 3 for about 25 minutes, until crisp and golden brown. Sprinkle with chopped parsley before serving.

CHEESE SAUCE: Use the strained hot milk from poaching the fish to make this sauce. Melt the butter in a pan and stir in the flour to make a roux. Cook gently over low heat for a couple of minutes, then gradually beat in the hot milk with a wooden spoon. Bring to the boil, stirring and beating until thickened. Then reduce the heat and simmer (on very low heat) for at least 10 minutes to let the sauce 'develop'. Don't forget to stir the sauce frequently with a wooden spoon to prevent it sticking to the pan. Add the grated Cheddar and a dollop of Dijon mustard.

FOR THE CHEESE SAUCE

50 g/2 oz butter
50 g/2 oz plain flour
reserved milk from poaching fish
180 g/6 oz mature Cheddar, grated
1 heaped teaspoon Dijon mustard

" *As a youngster, Nick was given this fish pie very regularly, as it was the only dish his mother could cook. With the passing of time, he now remembers it fondly.* "

MUSHROOM
STUFFED RAVIOLI

FOR THE PASTA

250 g/9 oz pasta flour ('grano duro' or 'hard wheat'), sifted with 1 1/2 teaspoons salt

3 eggs, beaten

2 tablespoons olive oil

melted butter and Parmesan cheese, to serve

NOSH TIP

To make eggwash, simply blend 1 egg yolk with 50 ml/2 fl oz milk.

*T*he trick here is to use stock cubes that don't make the stuffing mix mushy. Rolling the pasta thinly helps to keep the dish from being over-heavy. Most people don't attempt to make their own pasta — but it's so easy even the Italians can do it! Try this one at home.

RAVIOLI: Process all the ingredients together, except the melted butter and Parmesan cheese. Alternatively, if making the pasta by hand, mix the flour, salt, eggs and oil together, kneading it until it forms a soft dough. Divide into 3 pieces, if rolling out by hand, or into 6, if using a rolling machine. Roll out on a floured board to the thickness of a five-pence piece, then fold into three and roll slightly thinner. Repeat this process about 6 times, making the dough thinner each time. (Remember to keep the remainder of the dough covered whilst rolling the rest).

If using a machine, follow the instructions, feeding the small 'balls' of dough through the rollers and adjusting the thickness control to achieve a thin sheet. (Don't pull the sheets through, otherwise they will 'tear' and shred.)

Lay the finished sheets of pasta out on a floured clean tea towel — don't overlap them to avoid the danger of 'sticking together'. If the sheets dry slightly, this is helpful to the 'handling' process.

Opposite: Nosh fish pie (page 62).

To make ravioli by hand, you can use a pastry cutting wheel or simply use a scone cutter to make a round form.

Fill the ravioli with about one heaped teaspoon of filling to each 7.5-cm/3-in round, without over-filling. Seal the edges of the pasta with egg wash and sprinkle a little flour or semolina powder over the ravioli to prevent them sticking together.

Cook the ravioli in gently boiling lightly salted water. Note that fresh pasta takes only a few minutes to cook — about 3 minutes should be enough for 7.5-cm/3-in diameter ravioli. Avoid a violent boil or the pasta may split and leak. Serve the ravioli simply with melted butter (heat over a medium flame until nearly brown at the edge of the pan) and some grated fresh Parmesan and chopped parsley — or a sauce of your choice.

FILLING: Sweat the onion and garlic in 2 tablespoons of olive oil over a low heat for 20 minutes and reserve. Cook the mushrooms in the remaining olive oil over a low-medium heat, adding the half chicken stock cube, crumbled, until all the liquid has been 'reduced out' of the mushrooms. Then add the onion and garlic mixture, and combine. Process in a food processor for a few quick bursts to pulp the mixture — not too fine so as to leave some texture ('bite'). Stir in the black pepper, cheese and parsley.

FOR THE FILLING

1 small onion, finely chopped

1 garlic clove, chopped and crushed

6 tablespoons olive oil

225 g/8 oz closed cup mushrooms, thinly sliced

$1/2$ chicken stock cube (Knorr is good)

$1/2$ teaspoon freshly ground black pepper

3 tablespoons finely grated fresh Parmesan cheese

fresh parsley, chopped

NOSH TIP

When cutting rounds of pasta sheets, cut the 'top' discs slightly wider in diameter — to allow for the covering of the filling.

Opposite: Nosh coq au vin (page 56).

GRILLED DUCK
BREAST WITH FIG SAUCE

INGREDIENTS

350 g/12 oz dried figs

500 ml/16 fl oz dry sherry

1 cinnamon stick

pinch of ground cloves

1 star anise

2 duck carcasses for stock, with giblets

1 litre/1²/₃ pints chicken stock

500 ml/16 fl oz squeezed fresh orange juice

8 plump duck breasts

sea salt and freshly ground black pepper

melted butter for basting

P artly able to be pre-prepared the day before, this is a quick main course if you've made the stock and sauce beforehand.

METHOD: In a saucepan, soak the figs in the sherry with the cinnamon, pinch of cloves and star anise overnight.

Chop all the duck carcass bones and simmer in the chicken stock for 1 hour, ladling off the scum or any froth formed. Then reduce the stock to 500 ml/16 fl oz and strain.

Remove the cinnamon stick and star anise from the figs and add the stock. Simmer the figs gently on low heat until tender, then blitz in a blender. Return to the saucepan and add the orange juice. Boil gently to reduce to a thick sauce.

When required, preheat the oven to 220°C/425°F/Gas Mark 7. Season the breasts (trimmed prior of all sinews and 'flaps' of overhanging fat), brush with melted butter, and roast for

NOSH TIP

To seal in the juices firmly, each breast can be pan-fried first on all sides for a few minutes, just to 'seal' the flesh. Take care not to burn the skin side. Also, don't over-roast the breasts. Duck will dry out and be inedible if overdone.

15 minutes approximately, until cooked. Test for readiness by prodding to check rareness or, if you are nervous about judging it this way, insert a skewer to let the juices run and check to see if they are clear. If no pink is visible, then they 're ready.

Coat with the sauce and serve. A good accompaniment would be small roast potatoes with lemon juice squeezed over, and some fresh rosemary and leeks cooked plain and whole (without any extra sauces).

" *If you don't eat your meat... you can't get any pudding.* "

SQUIDS
STEWED IN INK

INGREDIENTS

1.8 kg/4 lb small squids, untrimmed weight

2 large Spanish onions, finely chopped

8 tablespoons good olive oil

5 garlic cloves, crushed

zest of 1/2 lemon, finely grated

25 g/1 oz fresh chopped parsley

50 g/2 oz fresh breadcrumbs

sea salt and freshly ground black pepper

1 small red chilli, seeded and finely chopped

600 ml/1 pint white wine

4 large plum tomatoes, skinned and chopped

1 teaspoon cornflour

dash of Armagnac

FOR COOKING

wooden cocktail sticks

Squid is really an underrated fish. It's not expensive, very nutritious and has a great taste, especially when very fresh. Freezing squid destroys all the appeal, rendering the fish rubbery and chewy, so don't be tempted to use any frozen stuff — wait until there's a fresh supply.

SQUIDS: Clean the squids by cutting off the tentacles at the head end just in front of the eyes. Pull off the eye/head section from the body and also the gut, discarding the eyes but leaving the dark ink sacs intact and undamaged, and the urn-shaped vessel of the body whole.

Remove the transparent 'plastic' bone from the body section and rinse out each body with cold water to remove any sand or entrails left. The squids are sometimes left with a dark purplish outerskin, which can be easily peeled off each body and discarded. The idea is to make a stuffing of the tentacles and stuff the bodies with this mixture.

STUFFING: Make the stuffing by cutting the cleaned tentacles and heads of the squids into small pieces. Fry half of the chopped onions in 4 tablespoons of the olive oil on a medium heat until softened. Add half of the garlic and all the chopped squid pieces and cook gently for 20 minutes.

Remove from the heat, add the lemon zest, parsley,

breadcrumbs and seasoning. Combine well and stuff the mix into the squid bodies.

Heat the remaining oil in a frying pan and lightly brown the squids together on each side, with the remaining garlic and onion and the chilli. Add the wine and tomatoes and simmer for about 30 minutes.

Next, pour the ink sacs' contents into a small bowl, add the cornflour and mix well together. (It will, of course, be quite black.) Stir it briskly into the sauce and season with salt and black pepper and the generous dash of Armagnac. Simmer on a very low heat, with the lid on, for 3/4-1 hour. Adjust the seasoning before serving if necessary — it should be an exceptionally strongly flavoured and memorable dish.

As the squids in their ink are such a full-on flavoured and substantial dish, we recommend that you need only serve them with mixed green salad and crusty bread to mop up the sauce.

SALAD: In a large bowl, mix some small washed and drained leaves of oak leaf, cos, mache (corn salad or sometimes called 'lambs lettuce'), Webbs, Romaine, Batavia or other similar crisp lettuces. Lollo Rosso, the frilly red lettuce so favoured by supermarket managers, has no place here or, indeed, anywhere in this book. Enough said. For the dressing we suggest a vinaigrette with a few chopped sun-dried tomatoes added.

NOSH TIP

To ensure the stuffing does not emerge from the squid bodies, thread wooden cocktail sticks through the opening of each squid to seal the opening. Don't forget to remove the sticks prior to serving.

desserts

SPICED APPLE STRUDEL

PANCAKES WITH
CHOCOLATE SAUCE

PLUM PUDDING WITH CASSIS

CHERRY CLAFOUTIS

AMERICAN BREAKFAST CAKE

BREAD AND BUTTER PUDDING
WITH WHISKY

PEAR TARTE TATIN

LEMON ZEST TART

TREACLE TART

BANOFFEE PIE

CLASSIC SHERRY TRIFLE

CREME BRULEE

CHOCOLATE MOUSSE WITH DARK RUM

BAKED RICE PUDDING WITH COCONUT

BAKED APPLES WITH
SPICES AND BLACKBERRIES

SPICED
APPLE STRUDEL

INGREDIENTS

1.4 kg/3 lb Bramley cooking apples

juice of 1 lemon, squeezed halves retained

2 cloves

1 small cinnamon stick

115 g/4 oz caster sugar

zest of 1 orange

50 g/2 oz sultanas

75 g/3 oz unsalted butter, melted

1 large packet fresh filo (strudel) pastry

icing sugar, for dusting

whipping cream mixed with kirsch (cherry eau-de-vie), to taste

This type of dessert had its origins in the Ottoman cuisine of the Middle East, but over the centuries migrated through into Europe. Popular in the Seventies when filo pastry became fashionable, we have always been fond of the flaky crust with a spicy sweet interior so it deserves a mention here. Filo, like many other Seventies efforts, is enjoying a little renaissance in food fashion, so we can put this recipe in with a clear conscience.

METHOD: First of all, preheat the oven to 200–225°C/ 400–425°F/Gas Mark 6–7.

Peel and core the apples, putting them in water with the squeezed lemon halves to avoid discolouration. Drain the apples well, then chop.

Put the lemon juice, apples, spices, sugar, orange zest and sultanas into a suitable pan. Cook over a low heat, stirring frequently to prevent the apples sticking and to encourage the

NOSH TIP

Don't assemble the strudel 'log' or 'parcels' more than 15 minutes before it is time for baking, otherwise the filo will get waterlogged and mushy.

juices to emerge from the apples as they cook down. The resulting stewed fruit mix should be quite stiff, with some chunks of apple visible and should not be a sloppy purée, otherwise it will not fill the strudel leaves easily. Take care as Bramleys will go to pulp easily if you overcook them. Remove the cloves and cinnamon stick.

When the fruit is ready, after about 5–8 minutes or so, butter each of the leaves of filo, placing one on top of each other in layers, and fill with the apple mixture in a long log down the central line of the pastry. Then fold the leaves of filo over the top of the fruit and create a log of pastry, tucking the ends of the filo inside the fold at each end. The butter that has been brushed on will tend to congeal as it cools and form a glue seal which should prevent any fruit escaping.

When the filling is already done, you only need to place the strudel in the oven, with the outside surface buttered generously, for 5–6 minutes or so, until browned in places. It is possible to make smaller individual 'parcels' of strudel, but you will need to watch the timing more closely to prevent over-baking. The hot strudel can be dusted with icing sugar and then cut into sections to be served with kirsch cream.

NOSH TIP

Try to get about six layers of filo per dessert. Too little and there will not be enough to cover the fruit. Too many layers, and the inner ones will not cook through crisply and will taste papery and 'wet' in the middle.

PANCAKES
WITH CHOCOLATE SAUCE

275 ml/9 fl oz full cream milk

2 tablespoons cocoa powder

275 ml/9 fl oz double cream

75 g/3 oz caster sugar

6 egg yolks

60 g/2¹/₂ oz dark luxury chocolate

25 ml/1 fl oz Grand Marnier liqueur

Traditionally, English pancakes are made rather thick to go with lemon juice and sugar for Shrove Tuesday. The recipe here calls for thinnish versions which can be cooked, then chilled and kept for assembling later. This is an ideal dish for preparing the day before.

CHOCOLATE SAUCE: Blend a little milk with the cocoa until it is a smooth paste, then mix into the rest of the milk. Heat the cream until it is nearly boiling, stirring until smooth. Whisk the sugar and yolks together and when the cream comes up to the boil pour in half, whisking well.

Pour the combined egg and cream mixture with the cocoa milk mix into a clean pan and continue to whisk. Turn the heat down to minimum and, using a wooden spoon, stir for about

NOSH TIP

To ensure that your pancakes will not stick, heat the pan up with some sunflower oil and wipe the metal suface with kitchen paper until all the oil has been 'burnt off' and 'seasons' the surface, making it non-stick. Do not wash your pancake pan in detergent ever!

4–5 minutes until the mix starts to thicken. (Do not overheat or the mixture will turn to 'scrambled eggs'.)

Remove from the heat, pass through a fine sieve into a jug, break in the chocolate chunks and stir gently until they melt. Add a generous dash of liqueur, then cool and chill until needed. When serving hot on pancakes, ensure that you reheat the mixture only gently, otherwise it will 'split'.

PANCAKES: Whisk the eggs and sugar into the milk until dissolved. Add a pinch of salt, and stir in the flour until you have a smooth batter. Melt the butter gently in a frying pan and pour out the melted butter into the batter and stir. Let it rest for 10 minutes.

Cook the pancakes in the usual way over a medium hot flame and turn with a palette knife. The finished pancakes should have a pale colour with golden-brown 'highlights' — do not overcook on the 'second side'. Fill with chocolate sauce and fold into quarters. Serve with whipped cream or ice cream.

FOR THE PANCAKES

2 eggs

25 g/1 oz caster sugar

300 ml/^{1}/$_2$ pint milk (slightly soured milk is fine)

pinch of salt

75 g/3 oz self-raising flour

50 g/2 oz unsalted butter

whipped cream, to serve

" This is an easy, filling dessert, which can be prepared the day before. "

PLUM PUDDING
WITH CASSIS

INGREDIENTS

**Sugar syrup
(made with 600 ml/1 pint dessert
wine and 2 tablespoons sugar)**

900 g/2 lb firm dark plums

large dash Cassis

6 tablespoons pudding rice

1.2 litres/2 pints milk

2 tablespoons sugar

6 drops vanilla essence

1 tablespoon gelatine

2 tablespoons cold water

**10 tablespoons plum syrup (from
poaching fruits)**

150 ml/5 fl oz double cream

2 egg whites, whipped until stiff

NOSH TIP

Line the moulds with clingfilm
before filling them — this will
make them easier to turn out.

A *moulded dessert with poached plums — not to be confused
with the Christmas-style plum pudding.*

METHOD: Make the syrup. Halve the plums and poach them
in the syrup gently for 8-10 minutes or so until tender. Add the
Cassis then allow to cool.

Wash the rice, drain and cook with the milk until tender,
stirring from time to time, to prevent sticking. Remove from heat,
add the sugar, vanilla essence and cool in a basin.

Soak the gelatine in the 2 tablespoons of water then add
the plum syrup. Melt the gelatine over a gentle flame and add to
the cooled rice mixture. Whip the cream until thickened and fold
the stiffened egg whites into it. Fold this into the rice cream
mixture.

Pour or spoon into dessert (Savarin-type) moulds, cover
with clingfilm and leave to set in a fridge.

To serve, drain the plums from the syrup. Turn out the rice
puddings onto plates and place plums on top, spooning over the
syrup. Any 'spare' plums may be skinned and sieved through a fine
sieve and the resulting coulis spooned around the edge of the puddings.

CHERRY CLAFOUTIS

SERVES 4-6

A traditional peasant dish which is basically cherries baked in a sweet custardy batter. We have added our own improvement with a touch of Cognac. It's important to use the correct size baking dish when making clafoutis — too large and the layer will dry out and not 'meet' the edges correctly; too small and the depth of the pudding will be too much with cherries piled on top of one another. There should be enough room in the dish for it to contain all the cherries in a single layer so that the custard batter sets all around the fruit evenly.

METHOD: Generously grease the inside surfaces of a large shallow baking dish (a lasagne-type large dish is perfect for this) with some of the softened butter. Arrange the cherries evenly around the dish in a single layer. Don't remove the cherry pits.

Make the batter by whisking the remaining butter and egg yolk in a bowl with the whole eggs, sugar and salt. Continue whisking until it has a smooth consistency. Whisk in the sifted flour and then the milk to make a smooth batter. Add a generous dash of Cognac and gently pour the batter over the cherries.

Bake uncovered in a medium hot preheated oven at 190°C/375°F/Gas Mark 5 for 35–40 minutes, or until it is puffed up and golden brown. Remove from the oven and allow to cool slightly. Sprinkle with vanilla sugar and serve straight from the baking dish with whipped cream.

INGREDIENTS

75 g/3 oz unsalted butter, softened

900 g/2 lb ripe black cherries, de-stalked

1 egg yolk

3 eggs (medium size)

175 g/6 oz caster sugar

pinch of salt

75 g/3 oz sifted plain flour

300 ml/¹/₂ pint whole milk

25 ml/1 fl oz Cognac (about 1 eggcupful)

3 teaspoons vanilla sugar, to serve

whipped cream, to serve

NOSH TIP

Vanilla sugar can easily be made at home by steeping 3 or 4 dried vanilla pods in a jar of caster sugar for a few weeks (see page 81 for the method).

AMERICAN
BREAKFAST CAKE

INGREDIENTS

300 g/10 oz plain flour

25 g/1 oz caster sugar

3 teaspoons baking powder

a pinch of salt

115 g/4 oz slightly salted butter, softened

50 g/2 oz mild Cheddar cheese, grated

milk to moisten

5 eating apples (Braeburn are good)

75 g/3 oz soft brown sugar

1 teaspoon powdered cinnamon

a little melted butter

This dessert can also be served and enjoyed with a good coffee (Guatemalan is our current favourite) at breakfast time or mid-morning. We are grateful to Mother N. Nosh for the inspiration for this recipe.

METHOD: Sieve the flour, caster sugar, baking powder and salt together into a bowl. Rub in the butter, then mix in the cheese. Add enough milk to moisten the mixture and form a soft but not sticky dough. Knead the dough lightly on a floured board. Pat it out on to an ungreased Swiss roll tin, about 18 x 25 cm/7 x 10 in.

Pare, core and thinly slice the apples, and arrange them generously on the dough. Sprinkle with the brown sugar and cinnamon, then brush with the melted butter, and bake in a preheated oven at 220°C/425°F/Gas Mark 7 for 25 minutes. Serve the breakfast cake warm.

NOSH TIP

When assembling the topping, arrange the apple slices in generous overlaps, otherwise the cake will be light on fruit flavour.

BREAD AND BUTTER
PUDDING WITH WHISKY

INGREDIENTS

300 ml/1/2 pint whole milk

8 tablespoons vanilla sugar

8 egg yolks

300 ml/1/2 pint single cream

3 tablespoons orange marmalade

a dash of whisky (a plain, non-peaty flavoured one)

a handful of raisins

1 loaf sliced white bread, crusts cut off

225 g/8 oz unsalted butter, melted

half a 450 g/1 lb jar apricot jam, sieved

Don't put raisins on top of the pudding. They will bake too hard — the result will be that the raisins will burn to a black colour and taste bitter, making them inedible. Nevertheless, this is a classic English pudding that is improved by a splosh of hooch!

METHOD: Start the custard by bringing the milk to the boil, then dissolving in it 6 tablespoons of the vanilla sugar. If you do not have vanilla sugar to hand, use caster sugar with the addition of 2 teaspoons vanilla essence. Set aside.

Whisk the egg yolks into the single cream with the marmalade and the whisky, and add this mix to the boiled milk, whisking vigorously together.

Grease the inside of a large oval gratin dish (a cast-iron Le Creuset type is good) with a little of the butter and sprinkle half of the raisins over the bottom. (This helps to create an easy way of lifting the portions out to serve.) Now cut the slices of bread into triangular quarters, and dip one side of the bread into the melted butter. Make a layer of triangles of buttered bread inside the dish, propping each one up against another so they are leaning slightly at an angle. (This will allow the custard mix to flow down between the layers and penetrate and cook evenly.) Now sprinkle the remaining raisins over the layer and arrange another layer of butter-dipped bread going the other way. Finish off with a third layer of bread, again arranged in the opposite direction. Pour the custard mix over slowly, ensuring that each top piece is soaked, and rest the pudding for 15 minutes to allow the fluid to settle and penetrate the whole dish.

Sprinkle over the remaining vanilla sugar and bake in a medium-hot preheated oven at 180°C/350°F/Gas Mark 4 for about 30–35 minutes. The position in the oven can be quite critical if you don't have a fan oven. The top of the pudding should be golden brown, with the bread quite crisp in parts. Conversely, the inner texture should be moist, soft and light, like a soufflé, but not runny. If in doubt, move the dish up or down accordingly. The second shelf down may be a good starting position.

Finally, when the pudding is taken out, brush the surface with warmed apricot jam to give it a good shine. This dessert can be served hot or even tepid, but loses its appeal when cooler. If you find you haven't had enough cholesterol, serve with clotted cream.

VANILLA SUGAR

Vanilla pods are quite expensive to buy in the UK, but their delicate flavour can be made good use of by splitting a couple of pods down one side and placing them in a jam jar with a screw-top lid, then filling up to near the top with caster sugar. The vanilla oils will permeate the sugar in a couple of days and within the week the flavour and aroma will be quite strong. Use to sprinkle on top of puddings and to flavour custards and ice creams.

PEAR
TARTE TATIN

See photograph opposite page 96.

See photograph opposite page 96.

INGREDIENTS

225 g/8 oz caster sugar

115 ml/4 fl oz water

90 g/3¹/₂ oz slightly salted butter

12 large, firm, under-ripe pears, peeled and cored, cut into quarters

2 x 225-g/8-oz blocks of fresh puff pastry (good quality, frozen will be fine), rolled out 5 mm/¹/₄ in thick

NOSH TIP

Keep a close eye on the bubbling fruits. They need to cook thoroughly but ensure that the caramel doesn't burn and turn bitter.

For this recipe you will need at least one metal-handled cast-iron frying pan, about 22.5–25 cm/9–10 in in diameter. It is unlikely that you will have a large enough pan or stove to make an eight-portion tart, so you'll have to have two pans (or, at least, make this dessert in two attempts).

METHOD: In a clean heavy-based frying pan, dissolve the sugar in a quarter of the water over a low heat and then turn up the flame to high to caramelize the sugar, adding the remaining water when the sugar begins to turn to caramel — the sugar will start to turn browner with that distinctive toffee aroma.

Don't overcook the sugar, otherwise it will turn blackish and bitter, in which case you will have to throw it away and start again!

Nearing the 'toffee-like' caramel spot, add the butter in small pieces, and stir it in; arrange the quarters of pear in the pan in a circle with the 'tops' pointing inwards. Continue to cook the fruits, browning them on a medium-high heat, in the caramel for about 5–10 minutes, until cooked but not mushy.

Take the pan off the heat and place a disc of pastry (cut 2.5 cm/1 in wider than the pan diameter and previously chilled in the freezer for at least 10 minutes) over the pears. Carefully tuck in the flap of 'spare' pastry under the pears.

Place in a hot preheated oven at 200°C/400°F/Gas Mark 6

for about 10–12 minutes, until the pastry has risen and is baked golden-brown.

Remove the pan, taking care to use a thick heat-insulating cloth to protect your hands, and allow to rest for 1–2 minutes. Then loosen the edge of the pastry with a sharp knife. With a large retaining plate on top of the tart, upturn the pan (don't forget the cloth!) and allow the tart to flip over onto the plate so that the fruit is now visible as the top of the tart.

The pears should have a brown coloration where they have been cooking in the sauce which should be sticky and cover the entire surface generously. Don't worry if any pears come unstuck on the pan — simply take them off with a palette knife and 'glue them' into place again.

" *Many know of the reputation of the Tatin sisters as perfectors of this dish, but not many have heard of their exchange student house guest 'Kevin Nosh' who, in error, made the fruit pie with the pastry on the wrong side. The rest is history.* "

LEMON ZEST TART

FOR THE PASTRY

300 g/10 oz plain flour

115 g/4 oz icing sugar

25 g/1 oz ground almonds

175 g/6 oz unsalted butter, softened and diced

2 egg yolks

a pinch of sea salt

a couple of drops of vanilla essence

grated zest of 2 lemons

plain flour for dusting

eggwash (1 yolk plus 1 tablespoon whole milk)

FOR THE FILLING

10 medium eggs

400 g/14 oz caster sugar

grated zest and juice of 5 lemons (unwaxed)

350 ml/12 fl oz fresh double cream

icing sugar and clotted cream, to serve

This pastry is essentially a shortbread dough which, although very fragile, has a beautiful texture and an incomparable taste. This recipe is a classic example of a fine English dish that the French stole and renamed as Tarte au Citron. Shun their inferior efforts and avoid all imitations.

PASTRY: Sift the flour, sugar and almonds together on to a board or clean smooth worktop, and make a well in the centre. Put the cubes of butter into the well with the egg yolks and work together with your hands. Add the salt, vanilla and lemon zest, and mix the pastry well together into a smooth-textured ball. Wrap in a polythene bag and chill in the fridge for 1 hour. Do not overwork the dough, otherwise it will become stiff and difficult to work with.

Preheat the oven to 200°C/400°F/Gas Mark 6. Roll out the pastry on a well-floured board to a thickness of 3 cm/1 1/4 in. Grease and flour a 25-cm/10-in flan tin. Place the pastry carefully in the tin, and trim the top edge to leave about 5 mm/1/4 in above the top edge of the flan tin. Chill in the fridge for about 30 minutes (this will stop the pastry collapsing during the first 5 minutes in the oven).

Bake blind, lined carefully with silicone baking parchment and baking beans, in the preheated oven for 15 minutes. Remove the flan tin from the oven, take out the paper and beans, and brush the interior with eggwash. This will seal the pastry against cracks and prevent any filling leaking out. Now return to the oven at the slightly lower temperature of 150°C/300–325°F/Gas Mark 2–3 for another 5 minutes, until the glaze is slightly golden brown.

FILLING: Break the eggs into a bowl with the sugar and blend until smooth. Next, add the lemon zest and the juice. Whisk the cream lightly until slightly thickened, with a homogenized texture, and add to the eggs. Stir everything together and then pour into the finished flan case. Bake in the oven at 150–160°C/300–325°F/Gas Mark 2–3 for about 1–1 1/4 hours, until the filling has set.

When ready, take out of the oven. Remove the outer ring, and slide a palette knife gently under the pastry to release the tart from the metal base. This pastry is very fragile so take great care. Serve the tart sprinkled with icing sugar. Accompany with clotted cream, if desired.

NOSH TIP

Traditionally, this tart is served cool, but beware, the pastry will get soggy if kept chilled in a fridge. Store it in a cool place.

" Here's a fine example of a great English pudding hijacked by the French and paraded as their own. We say, 'Remember Agincourt'. "

TREACLE TART

SERVES 6-8

FOR THE PASTRY

225 g/8 oz plain flour

pinch of salt

150 g/5 oz unsalted butter, diced

4 teaspoons caster sugar

4 tablespoons iced water

2 egg yolks

FOR THE FILLING

1 medium tin golden syrup

grated zest and juice of 1 lemon

16 heaped tablespoons fresh breadcrumbs

1 tablespoon freshly grated and pulped root ginger

Fondly remembered as a childhood favourite, we have added some fresh ginger to give an added zing to the mix. Adults can now experience culinary déja vu.

PASTRY: Sift the flour and salt into a bowl and work in the butter with your fingertips until the mixture resembles fine breadcrumbs. Stir in the caster sugar. Mix 3 tablespoons of iced water and the egg yolks together, and then stir into the pastry mixture. Mix to a firm dough, adding more water if necessary, but don't get the mix too 'wet'.

Roll out the pastry 5 mm/¼ in thick and use to line a greased, floured 25-cm/10-in pie dish. Prick the pastry lightly, taking care not to puncture the base right through.

FILLING: Warm the syrup to a flowing consistency and add the lemon zest and juice and the breadcrumbs with the ginger. Pour into the pastry case and bake in a preheated oven at 180°C/350°F/Gas Mark 4 for about 30–40 minutes, until the pastry edge is almost browned. The filling will go quite chewy if left until completely cold so ensure that you serve this tart on the warm side. Traditionally, it is enjoyed with custard.

BANOFFEE PIE

225 g/8 oz plain chocolate Hobnob biscuits, crushed into crumbs

175 g/6 oz unsalted butter, melted

3 x 225-g/8-oz cans sweetened condensed milk

4 large ripe bananas

1 teaspoon Demerara sugar

freshly grated zest of 1 lemon

300 ml/¹/₂ pint double cream

115 g/4 oz plain chocolate, grated

This has got to be one of the richest and stickiest puddings ever. We have improved this Eighties' favourite by using the extra richness and texture of chocolate Hobnobs as a biscuit base.

METHOD: Line the base of a 25-cm/10-in springform cake tin with greaseproof paper. Mix the chocolate Hobnob crumbs with the melted butter and then press the crumb mixture down lightly into the bottom of the lined tin to a depth of about 5 mm/¹/₄ in to form the pie crust base.

NOSH TIP

It is very important that you watch closely when the cans of condensed milk are simmering away. Keep checking that they are totally covered in water to avoid a minor explosion in your kitchen! The heat from the water will caramelize the sugar in the milk in the cans and turn it into a brown sticky toffee. Delicious!

Immerse the cans of condensed milk in a pan of boiling water and simmer, unopened, for 1½–2 hours. Ensure that the cans are covered completely all the time, or they will burst and shower the kitchen with boiling toffee! Cool a little, and then spoon the warm toffee out of the cans on to the biscuit base. Spread it evenly to a depth of about 1 cm/½ in. Use a palette knife for this, dipping it in hot water to ensure that it coats evenly.

Peel and slice the bananas and arrange them in a thin layer on top of the toffee. Whisk the lemon zest into the cream, then continue beating until stiff. Spread a layer of whipped cream over the bananas, covering the whole surface of the pie. For the finishing touch, sprinkle some freshly grated chocolate over the top. Turn out the pie and serve cut into slices.

> " *A strange dessert – the biscuit and condensed milk have a whiff of war-time austerity. Despite this, with the Nosh twist it has made the grand transition from 'Chalet-girl' repertoire to restaurant offering.* "

CLASSIC
SHERRY TRIFLE

FOR THE NUT BRITTLE

175 g/6 oz flaked almonds

50 g/2 oz caster sugar

25 g/1 oz unsalted butter

FOR THE TRIFLE

8 small trifle sponges

150 ml/¹/₄ pint sweet cream or oloroso sherry

175 g/6 oz pecan nuts, freshly shelled and halved

450 g/1 lb fresh ripe raspberries

2 blocks raspberry jelly

2 ripe bananas

1.8 litres/3 pints vanilla custard

600 ml/1 pint double cream

This is another of those typical English desserts that we take for granted. Made properly, it has the power to make foreigners swoon at their first taste. Although it is not usually associated with wintry images, we consider it tailor-made for this book as a breath of summer air. We have experimented with different types of sponge and cakes, some fresh and some slightly dry. Most work quite well, even chocolate ones, but the important thing is to ensure that the layer of cake is well soaked in alcohol and is moist.

NUT BRITTLE: Make the nut brittle for the topping first to give it time to cool down. Heat a clean, dry frying pan over a medium heat and swirl the flaked almonds around for a few minutes, until they start to colour up a golden brown, tossing frequently to avoid burning. Add the sugar, stirring until it has heated up, and then add the butter. Cook the sugar and butter mix, stirring frequently until it changes to a sticky toffee and has a caramel aroma. Take care not to burn the nuts.

This mixture will become a sugary lump which can be spooned out on to a sheet of greaseproof paper to cool. When cold, it will resemble peanut brittle and can be crumbled up into small lumps for the topping. While the nut brittle is cooling, you can assemble the trifle.

TRIFLE: Place the cake sponges around the sides and base of a large glass trifle bowl. Pour the sherry evenly over the top to dampen the sponges. Sprinkle half of the pecans around the bowl and tip in all the raspberries, discarding any berries that show signs of fur.

Chill in the freezer for 15 minutes. Then when the jelly is poured in, the molten jelly will set in a layer and not soak into the moist sponges.

Dissolve the jelly cubes in 300 ml/^{1}/$_2$ pint hot water then add 300 ml/^{1}/$_2$ pint cold water when dissolved. Allow to cool. When the jelly is starting to set, pour it over the sponge layer. Replace in the fridge for at least 1 hour, until the jelly sets firm. Slice the bananas over the top and then pour over the cold custard, smoothing the top flat with a rubber spatula. Spread the remaining pecans over the top.

Whip the double cream until stiff peaks form. Spread a layer of cream over the trifle, at least 1 cm/^{1}/$_2$ in thick. Lastly, sprinkle with the nut brittle and chill the pudding in the fridge for 1 hour before serving. This will allow the fruits to settle and the sponge to soak up all the juices completely.

Not usually associated with wintry images, trifle is tailor-made for this book as a breath of fresh air.

CREME **BRULEE**

INGREDIENTS

600 ml/1 pint double cream

3 vanilla pods, split

8 egg yolks

2 tablespoons caster sugar

2 punnets fresh raspberries

unsalted butter for greasing

Demerara sugar for caramel lid

Another traditional idea we've livened up with fresh fruits in the base. We've adapted this from our relative, Uncle Mortimer Nosh's famous invention. As a Spitfire pilot called to action at short notice, he kept a supply of these splendid desserts on him in chilled ramekins for those peckish patrol moments.

METHOD: Place the cream and the vanilla pods in a high-sided saucepan. Heat slowly, stirring occasionally, to just below · boiling point (don't let the cream boil). Set aside to cool slightly for 5 minutes. Remove the vanilla pods.

Now preheat the oven to 160–180°C/325–350°F/Gas Mark 3–4. Whisk the egg yolks with the sugar until creamy in consistency, and then stir in the warm cream.

NOSH TIP

It is important when cooking the ramekins of creamy custard to fit the foil lids exactly. If the foil drops down below the water level in the bain-marie, steam and water may 'bubble' up under the lids and spoil the mixture by dilution.

Grease 8 ramekins and line the bottom of each one with fresh raspberries, then fill with the mixture to about 1cm/^{1}/$_2$ in from the top lip. Place foil squares over the pots and smooth down the sides so the foil lid is straight and level, i.e. not touching the mixture.

Place the ramekins, evenly spaced, into a hot water bain-marie and cook in the preheated oven for 15–17 minutes. Test one after 15 minutes by peeking in under the foil lid and gently tapping to check its solidity: prod the surface gently with your finger (don't break the skin of the custard), and ascertain whether it's too sloppy and needs another few minutes. Allow to cool, then refrigerate. The brûlées can be prepared up to this point the day before. Uncover and sprinkle a generous layer of sugar, 3–5 mm/^{1}/$_8$–^{1}/$_4$ in thick, evenly over the entire surface.

Preheat the grill to its maximum until it is red-hot, and then get the ramekins as close to the heat as possible. Watch the sugar melting and turning into caramel. You have to remove the pots immediately to stop the cream layer underneath boiling. Turn the pots around and rotate the less brown areas to catch the heat best. Allow to cool completely before serving.

NOSH TIP

Do not use soft brown muscovado-type sugar as this burns black without caramelizing properly.

> " *Literally 'burnt cream', this was invented by our Uncle Mortimer Nosh who was a gourmet and Spitfire pilot. His love of old English recipes was thwarted by the French who stole his invention and renamed it. A writ is pending.* "

CHOCOLATE MOUSSE
WITH DARK RUM

300 g/10 oz luxury dark Continental chocolate (75 per cent cocoa solids)

4 tablespoons caster sugar

3 egg yolks, at room temperature

7 egg whites, at room temperature

a large dash of strong dark rum

50 g/2 oz unsalted butter, softened

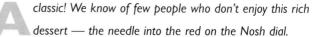

classic! We know of few people who don't enjoy this rich dessert — the needle into the red on the Nosh dial.

METHOD: Break the chocolate into little squares and place in a bowl over some gently simmering hot water to melt them. Do not overheat or you'll coagulate the chocolate. Whisk half of the sugar with the egg yolks until smooth and creamy. Then, with a clean dry whisk, whisk the whites until stiff and foamy, and then add the remaining sugar to the whites and continue to whisk together. The secret here is to add the sugar towards the end, otherwise, if added too early, the whites will not stiffen into peaks. On the addition of the sugar the peaks will take on a glossy look and you should then add the rum. Then divide the egg whites between three separate dishes.

NOSH TIP

- Do not add liqueur to the chocolate directly.
- Do not overheat the chocolate.
- Do not attempt this dish with cheap inferior chocolate — it must be 50 per cent cocoa solids minimum.

Add the butter to the melted chocolate and remove the pan from the heat. Now the timing is crucial. Once cool materials are added to the chocolate mix, the mousse will start to solidify, so rapid whisking is required to avoid chocolate 'chips'.

First, fold the yolk mix into the first lot of whites and mix thoroughly but gently. Then add the chocolate mix quickly and fold thoroughly together to blend the chocolate without any 'chips' appearing.

Next, fold in the second batch of whites gently with a large spoon to give volume, and stir around. Then add the final batch, folding very gently to distribute the whites evenly and keep the mousse as light as possible. Work lightly with upward movements to get as much air as possible into the bowl, and don't overwork each stage. Stop as soon as the whites are fully incorporated. Spoon the mousse mixture neatly and quickly into a serving bowl, or some individual ramekins or dessert glasses, and refrigerate for a couple of hours before serving. This is such a 'full-on' recipe for mousse that you can pour it into egg cups and you will be surprised how filling it still is! Remove the mousse from the fridge 15 minutes or so before serving — it's best chilled but not so cold as to kill the flavour!

" The Aztecs revered chocolate as food worthy of the gods, and reserved it for royalty. The choc habit was imported to Europe by the Conquistadors — well done, Aztecs! "

BAKED **RICE PUDDING** WITH COCONUT

450 g/1 lb short-grain pudding rice

1.8 litres/3 pints whole milk

1 small can coconut milk

225 g/8 oz caster sugar

pinch of salt

butter, for greasing

1/2 teaspoon ground nutmeg

1/2 teaspoon ground mace

115 g/4 oz Demerara sugar

a little fresh grated coconut flesh

NOSH TIP

A baked rice pudding should have the same moist consistency as a bread and butter pudding, i.e. soft and gooey in the centre, with a firm top. Adjust the quantities of liquid according to the type of rice used.

*G*iven the Nosh twist of adding spices and coconut, this childhood favourite is transformed into a fabulous fusion of East meets West.

METHOD: Wash the rice in cold water to remove the chaff and drain thoroughly. In a large saucepan, bring the milk and coconut milk to the boil with the caster sugar, salt and rice, stirring frequently to prevent the rice 'catching' on the bottom of the pan.

Then, when boiled, transfer the rice pudding to an ovenproof ceramic 'lasagne-type' dish or a cast-iron gratin dish which has been generously buttered on all sides. If the rice looks too thick, stir in some more milk — it will absorb quite a bit. Sprinkle with the nutmeg and mace, and cover the dish with foil.

Bake the rice pudding in a medium-hot oven at 180°C/350°F/Gas Mark 6 for 25–30 minutes. Sprinkle the Demerara sugar finely all over the top and pop under a very hot grill for 5 minutes or so, until the sugar has melted and crisped up the topping. Decorate with a few gratings of fresh coconut.

Opposite: Pear tarte tatin (see page 82).

BAKED APPLES WITH SPICES AND BLACKBERRIES

Baked apples may sound a bit ordinary but trust us — with blackberries it's a great combination. It makes a quick and easy dessert when you're in a hurry.

METHOD: Marinate the raisins and fresh blackberries with the ground almonds in the rum with the lemon and orange zests and juice for 1 hour. Meanwhile, core the apples vertically with a circular corer, and score a horizontal line through the skin of each apple around the 'equator'. (This will prevent the apple splitting randomly during baking.)

Preheat the oven to 220°C/425°F/Gas Mark 7. After the marination time, add the sugar and spices to the fruit filling and mix together. Use to fill the hole in each apple. Arrange the stuffed apples on a roasting tray, put a good knob of butter on top of each one and pour the golden syrup lightly over each apple to cover the skin.

Pour 8 tablespoons of water into the dish to prevent sticking and dot any remaining butter in and around the dish. Bake in the preheated oven for 30–40 minutes. The apples should be cooked perfectly throughout but not falling apart and turning into jam. To help the process, baste occasionally with the pan juices, which will reduce slightly into a syrup. Place each apple on a warmed dessert plate and pour over the syrup. Serve with double cream.

Opposite: Baked apples with spices and blackberries.

INGREDIENTS

25 g/1 oz raisins

115 g/4 oz fresh blackberries, washed and drained

25 g/1 oz ground almonds

2 tablespoons rum

zest and juice of 1 lemon

zest and juice of 1 orange

8 large Bramley cooking apples

4 tablespoons Demerara sugar

1/2 teaspoon cinnamon

1/4 teaspoon allspice

2 tablespoons butter

2 tablespoons golden syrup

double cream, to serve

drinks

HOT CHOCOLATE
WITH RUM

SERVES 4

INGREDIENTS

600 ml/1 pint whole milk

2 teaspoons caster sugar

6 tablespoons hot chocolate powder

6 measures dark rum

whipped cream

ground cinnamon

cinnamon sticks for stirring

4 cubes dark chocolate (optional)

Mick first had this drink after skating on the frozen canals in Holland. Something of a tradition there, it is hard to get the skates back on after a few of these!

METHOD: Heat the milk and when it is hot, stir in the sugar until dissolved, then add the chocolate powder (Continental blends seem to have more choccy 'body' to them). Pour in the rum and then dispense into large mugs. Float whipped cream on each and sprinkle some cinnamon on top. Use cinnamon sticks to stir.

The addition of a cube of chocolate in each mug makes for a sticky ending at the bottom of the mug.

NOSH **BOSH**

SERVES 1

INGREDIENTS

1 flaming measure of Sambuca

1 large espresso

METHOD: The flaming Sambuca is poured into the hot espresso (whereby the flames are extinguished) and then drunk. As the liqueur is quite sweet, no sugar is needed in the coffee.

TRADITIONAL
GLUHWEIN

SERVES 16

This German-style mulled red wine is a traditional hot punch that has a real kick. Remember to add the brandy last to top up the alcohol level that has 'boiled off'.

METHOD: Cut the oranges and lemons in half, squeeze out the juice (lightly) into a large enamel casserole dish or pot, and stud the squeezed halves with cloves.

Then pour the red wine into the pot with the sugar, and mix the wine, juice and sugar together to dissolve the sugar in the liquid.

'Float' the squeezed, spiced fruits in the pot and add the cinnamon sticks, breaking them in half. Place the pot on a medium heat and bring to a high heat, without letting the brew boil, stirring occasionally to ensure that the sugar has dissolved properly. Then add the sherry, stir and, just before serving, add the brandy.

Don't keep the pot at a high constant heat — just let it stay warm (Le Creuset thick cast-iron enamelled pots are good for this). Usually the wine disappears before you need to reheat it!

If you want to make a fresh batch, you can leave the 'old' fruit and spices in, but don't forget that they will be partly 'spent' in their strength — so taste the glühwein as you go to ensure a robust mixture.

INGREDIENTS

3 oranges

2 lemons

12 cloves

4 bottles medium red wine

approx 115 g/4 oz caster sugar (or more to taste)

4 cinnamon sticks

$1/4$ bottle dry sherry

$1/4$ bottle French brandy

NOSH TIP

Remember that alcohol evaporates quickly above 80°C so add the brandy last to keep the 'kick' in. You can buy spice mixtures specially for mulled wine, already made up in muslin bags, with dried peels, and mixed spices. Try some differing brands and experiment.

MOOSEMILK
PUNCH

SERVES 20

6 eggs

113 g/4 oz caster sugar

2 litres/ 4¹/₂ pints milk

1 litre/2¹/4 pints vanilla ice cream, partially melted

600 ml/1 pint dark rum

400 ml/13 fl oz brandy

400 ml/13 fl oz Tia Maria

freshly grated nutmeg

A little Canadian moosemilk made from real mooses. It's not a hot drink — but it sure ain't a summer one!

METHOD: Separate the egg yolks and whites into separate bowls. Add the sugar to the yolks and beat until frothy. Beat the whites until they form peaks. Combine the yolk and white mixtures and add with the milk to the partially melted ice cream. Add the rum, brandy and Tia Maria last. Serve sprinkled with nutmeg.

NOSH TIP

Use a good-quality vanilla ice cream for this drink — Haagen Daaz or Rocombe Farms are both very good and will give good results.

VIRGIN
MARY

SERVES 5

This is a Nosh-style non-alcoholic drink for people who have 'taken the pledge' — baptists, dialysis patients, muslim fundamentalists, those on heavy medication, Jehova's Witnesses and the like.

METHOD: In a large jug, mix the juices and seasonings together. Place some ice cubes in some large tumblers and pour over a good measure. Stir around gently and add a stick of celery, if desired, for decoration.

NOSH TIP

This cocktail can easily be returned to normality and a good old-fashioned Bloody Mary by the addition of a large slug of good vodka.

INGREDIENTS

1 x 300-ml/¹/₂-pint can V8 vegetable juice

1-litre/1²/₃-pints carton premium tomato juice

juice of ¹/₂ lemon

juice of 1 lime

¹/₂ teaspoon fine freshly ground black pepper

²/₃ teaspoon celery salt

pinch of grated nutmeg

5 shakes Tabasco (or to taste)

7 shakes Worcestershire sauce

2 tablespoons horseradish sauce (1 only if strong)

celery sticks, for decoration (optional)

JULEGLØGG

SERVES 5-6

INGREDIENTS

peeled zest of $\frac{1}{2}$ orange and $\frac{1}{2}$ lemon

4 cloves

1 cinnamon stick

1 green cardamon pod

50 g/2 oz raisins

1 large glass (250 ml/8 fl oz) brandy French brandy

1 bottle full-bodied red wine

$\frac{1}{4}$ bottle port

115 g/4 oz soft brown sugar (or more to taste)

50 g/2 oz blanched, peeled almonds

We are indebted to Auntie Bente for her inspiration for this Danish-style hot punch called Gløgg but pronounced 'glugg'. Although, as she says, "Why can't you [boys] drink champagne like normal people?"

METHOD: Peel the orange and lemon zests lightly into a large enamel casserole with the spices, raisins and brandy. Leave for a few hours to soak. Then pour the red wine and port into the pot with the sugar, and mix the wine, spices and sugar together to dissolve the sugar in the liquid. Heat gently until hot but do not boil, stirring occasionally, to ensure that the sugar has dissolved properly. Serve in heatproof glasses with some almonds and raisins.

NOSH TIP

To serve, don't keep the pot over a high constant heat — just let it stay warm (thick cast-iron enamelled pots are good) and usually the wine disappears before you need to reheat it!

If you want to make a fresh batch, you can leave the 'old' fruit and spices in, but don't forget they will be partly 'spent' in their strength — so add to them as necessary and taste as you go along to ensure a robust mixture.

JEREZ COCKTAIL

SERVES 1

After Christmas you may have a few 'odd' bottles of drink hanging around which need finishing up. Sherry, although a fortified wine, doesn't stay fresh for more than a few weeks after opening. People who think they can make it last until next Christmas are much mistaken. Use up the back shelf of your cabinet with this one. It produces a fruity wine flavour.

METHOD: Half fill a tumbler with cracked ice and pour the spirits over, then stir to mix.

2 measures dry sherry (cream sherry if you must)

1 teaspoon peach brandy (or schnapps)

1 teaspoon triple sec

HEAD BUTT

SERVES 1

Like its Glaswegian cousin, this packs a strong punch. Concocted in a regular shaker, it uses fresh ginger to enliven the taste buds. Made with ice and poured into a large tumbler with rocks, it can be made 'longer' with the addition of soda or ginger ale.

METHOD: Peel the root ginger and slice thickly. Place in a cocktail shaker with the ice. Pour the Scotch over, cover and shake for a few moments. Strain out into an ice-filled glass. A very adult drink!

2.5-cm/1-in (approx) piece of fresh peeled root ginger, according to taste

4–5 ice cubes

2 measures blended Scotch whisky

BAILEYS ESPRESSO

SERVES 1

INGREDIENTS

1 large hot espresso (in a short demi-tasse cup)

double measure Baileys Irish Whiskey cream liqueur

METHOD: Simply pour the hot coffee into the liqueur. There is no need for extra sugar.

WHISKY MAC

SERVES 1

INGREDIENTS

1 measure good quality whisky

1 measure Stones ginger wine

METHOD: Simply combine the whisky and ginger wine in a glass (or jug if preparing in bulk) in equal quantities.

MARS ATTACKS

SERVES 1

INGREDIENTS

1 small carton Mars milk

large double measure of good brandy

whipped cream, to serve

METHOD: Warm the Mars milk in a non-stick saucepan and, when hot, add the brandy. Mars milk is quite a sweet drink and the addition of the brandy becomes a surprisingly good warmer! Top with whipped cream for an extra richness.

BRANDY AND
BENEDICTINE

SERVES 1

Like many drinks that can trace their pedigree back to the Middle Ages, Benedictine was invented by the Benedictine monks as a herbal remedy.

METHOD: Combine the brandy with the Benedictine to make a formidable winter warmer.

1 large measure good quality brandy

1 large measure Benedictine

CLASSIC
MARGARITA

SERVES 8

600 ml/1 pint lemon and lime juice (70% lemon; 30% lime)

1 litre/1³⁄₄ pints tequila (gold label is best)

Drinks play an important role as social lubricants. This classic Margarita is a great cocktail for festive winter parties, especially served with hot spicy food and nibbles.

METHOD: Mix the lemon and lime juice together with the tequila in a jug. Put some ice in some glasses and pour the Margarita mixture over the ice. After the second glass, you'll be well on your way! We don't recommend the addition of a salted glass rim, but it's down to personal choice.

When people ask us for advice on how to cure hangovers, we reply, 'We don't cure them, we give 'em!'

CIDER AND
BRANDY PUNCH

SERVES 6

INGREDIENTS

zest of 1 lemon and 1 orange

900 ml/1½ pints dry strong cider

50 g/2 oz soft brown sugar

2 cinnamon sticks

4 cloves

2 blades of mace, dried

2.5-cm/1-in slice of peeled root ginger

1 teaspoon grated nutmeg

3 tablespoons brandy

2 apples, cored and sliced

METHOD: Put the lemon and orange zest, cider, sugar and spices into a deep-sided pan and warm through for about 10 minutes. Add the brandy and reheat gently. Serve with sliced fresh apples.

Cheers !

INDEX